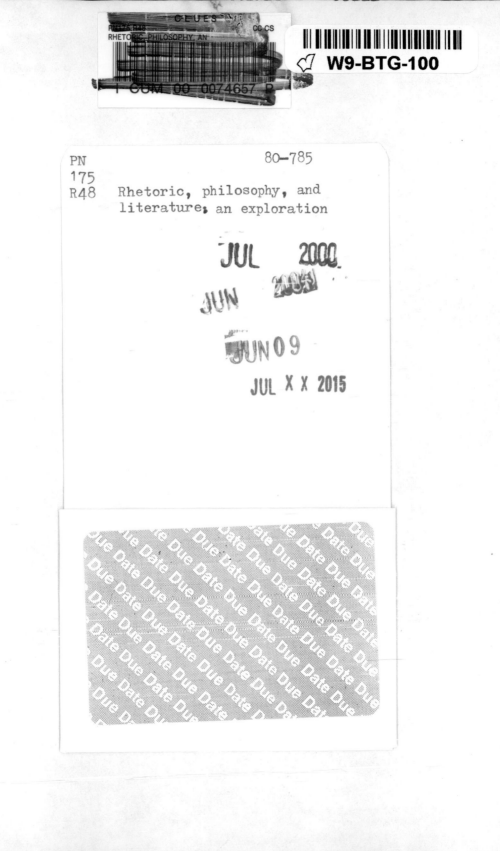

Rhetoric, Philosophy, and Literature:
An Exploration

Rhetoric, Philosophy, and Literature:

An Exploration

Edited by
Don M. Burks

1978
Purdue University Press
West Lafayette, Indiana

Library of Congress Catalog Card Number 77-92712
International Standard Book Number 0-911198-52-0
Printed in the United States of America

Dedication

This collection of essays in rhetoric, philosophy, and literature is dedicated to a rhetorician and to a philosopher: Frederick W. Haberman, Andrew T. Weaver Professor of Communication Arts, University of Wisconsin, "a good man, skilled in speaking," and Arthur Campbell Garnett (1894-1970), former professor of philosophy, University of Wisconsin, who taught a "simple theistic faith" with an eloquence both direct and indirect.

Contents

Preface

This collection of essays grew out of an interdisciplinary seminar held at Purdue University during the spring semester of 1974. Funded by the Office of the Dean of the School of Humanities, Social Science, and Education, the course was entitled Seminar in Rhetoric, Philosophy, and Literature. Six guest teachers were invited to present a public lecture and participate in the seminar during their separate visits. In addition to student members of the seminar, the larger audience for the lectures consisted primarily of students and teachers from the four departments supporting the seminar: Communication, English, Philosophy, and Political Science. The essays of this collection have evolved from the public lectures by the six invited teachers. Lloyd F. Bitzer and Kenneth Burke have in their essays added significantly to their lecture presentations. The essays by Wayne C. Booth and Donald C. Bryant are changed slightly from their lecture versions. The essays by Maurice Natanson and Henry W. Johnstone, Jr., are changed only in the most minor particulars from their lecture typescripts.

Within this collection the essays are arranged not in the order of their presentation as public lectures, but according to relationships that may be seen if the essays are read serially. The essays by Booth, Burke, and Natanson deal with indirect meaning and figurative language. The essays by Johnstone and Bitzer, though quite different from one another in approach, are concerned with the problem of validation and authorization. Natanson's essay is also suggestive on the problem of validation and may thus serve as a transition to the essays by Johnstone and Bitzer. Finally, Bitzer and Bryant share a concern with the relationship of politics and rhetoric.

References to rhetoric, either explicit or implicit, constitute the relationship most in evidence among the six essays. Although invitations to the guest teachers mentioned no specific theme for their lectures, the interdisciplinary aspect of the seminar with rhetoric as a unifying concept was suggested. Each author has long-standing interest in rhetoric, but their differing "home departments"—speech-communication, philosophy, English—indicate that rhetoric is the special province of no one department and an appropriate subject for an interdisciplinary seminar.

Preface

For any reader unfamiliar with rhetoric as a concept, there may be advantage in reading Bryant's essay first rather than last, for among his objectives herein is the confirming of a traditional view of rhetoric. To Bryant rhetoric is the "rationale of the informative and suasory in discourse," having "as its chief concern . . . 'adjusting ideas to people and people to ideas.'"[1] These two statements, the first in very slightly different form, have long been recognized among teachers of speech-communication as a succinct definition and statement of the function of rhetoric. It is this traditional concept in which rhetoric is seen "not as digests of devices but as a mode of approaching the phenomena of discourse"[2] that Bryant here reviews and confirms.

Of the six authors, Booth alone does not explicitly refer to the word "rhetoric." His essay is, nevertheless, a concise abridgment of his book *A Rhetoric of Irony*. In reviewing that book, Burke says, "By 'rhetoric' he [Booth] has in mind the ways whereby the use of irony establishes a bond of 'communion' between writer and reader. When a sentence would be interpreted one way if taken straight, quite as it says on the surface, and in a wholly different way if read with the proper ironic discount, then ironic writer and ironic reader are in league. They share a realm for which the literal-minded are self-excluded. This is what Booth seems to be saying."[3] In the lecture as recorded, Booth used the word "rhetoric" in a way that accords with what Burke says Booth has in mind. In the essay Booth writes, "The very intricacy of our interpretative act builds for us, when we manage to do it right, a tight bond with the author. . . ."[4] At that place in his lecture, Booth said, "The very intricacy of our interpretative act builds for us, when we manage to do it right, a kind of *rhetoric* which no straightforward speech can ever duplicate, I think, a tighter bond with the author than any other kind of *rhetoric* can achieve, except perhaps metaphoric—other kinds of metaphoric language. I think probably irony is the tightest of all when it works." Throughout his essay and his book, Booth seems to have in mind the question of how authors and readers achieve ironic meaning together. In his preface to *A Rhetoric of Irony*, Booth says this is "an exclusively rhetorical focus."[5] Such an understanding of the word "rhetorical" departs somewhat from a more traditional meaning; both Booth and Burke have in their works demonstrated familiarity with traditional Aristotelian usage, but both are freer in their own usages.

Students of rhetoric sometimes note that oral disclosure, not written disclosure, is the most characteristic dimension of the rhetorical, the word "rhetoric" being an anglicized form of the Greek word for public speaking.[6] Little is said in this collection of essays about that fact. Yet each essay was originally presented as a lecture, and for those who participated in the seminar, the oral dimension—discourse between the guest teachers and students of the seminar—was probably the paramount benefit. The informal evening seminars, the conferences between teacher and student, presented opportunities that can hardly be found from reading the written work of any writer. The guest teachers provided members of the seminar with privileged moments in communication. Even the more formal lecture situations presented the opportunity for everyone in the audience to see if he or she perceived incongruity between the speaker and his message. In that respect the most characteristic dimension of the rhetorical, orality, was indeed paramount in these interdisciplinary lectures in rhetoric, philosophy, and literature.

There is no need to continue here, however, one of the ironies in Plato's *Phaedrus* by belittling the written word in a book that demonstrates its lasting value. The six contributors have provided all the main thoughts presented in their public lectures for the seminar, so that no further prefatory statements are required. The reader may see that in a significant way, even if in a metaphorical way, it may be said that the contributors here speak for themselves, and they will long continue to do so.

Acknowledgments

Purdue University colleagues who wrote statements supporting the funding of this project are Ray Nadeau and Charles Redding of the Department of Communication, Jacob Adler and Harold Watts of the Department of English, Richard Grabau and Calvin Schrag of the Department of Philosophy, and Winfried Dallmayr of the Department of Political Science. Dean Leon Trachtman of the School of Humanities, Social Science, and Education was supportive throughout the project.

Special acknowledgment is due to Edwin Black, editor of *Quarterly Journal of Speech* (1975-77), for editorial suggestions concerning publication of this collection.

Students participating in the seminar were Elizabeth Davis, Gail Dixon, Diana Doyle, David Dries, Paul Feingold, Michael Hyde, Carol Jablonski, Theresa Kelley, Rebecca Leonard, Ann Marie Lovato, Douglas Morrison, Frederick Murphy, Shirley Quate, Catherine Quinn, Samuel Robinson, Joyce Schafer, James Walsh, and Stephen Young.

The Pleasures and Pitfalls of Irony:

or,
Why Don't You Say What You Mean?

Wayne C. Booth

I'm afraid that I have rather unpleasant news for us all. I'm not Wayne Booth but Wayne Booth's brother George from Chicago State Teacher's College. At the last minute Wayne Booth had to back out, or so he said when he called me, to ask if I'd take his place this afternoon, using his notes and my memory of conversations we've had together over the years. I didn't like the idea—all our lives he's been using me in this way. But he finally talked me into it. In case you're interested, we're not twins, but we look enough alike so that he thought I could fool you with the cooperation of faculty members like Don Burks who know Wayne Booth. I drew the line at that, being more honest than he is. Just as I was leaving, Wayne gave me a note which he didn't indend me to read to you. But since I feel sort of double-crossed by the whole deal, and know that you'll be disappointed by having to sit through a second-hand lecture, I owe it to you to read his offensive words.

Dear George:

I hope you'll make clear to the students and faculty of Purdue how much I regret not being able to talk with them on the 18th. I also hope that you'll tell Don Browks, or whatever his name is, that I know it is unfair to make last minute changes like this. You might mention to him that if he feels picked on, perhaps he could pay you less than they were going to pay me. Since the lecture is that old one I gave to the inmates at the state prison ten years ago, I won't insist on receiving more than half of what they originally offered, that is, $12.50, plus expenses, which in my case will be only seven cents for my call this morning and ten cents postage. You can take whatever is left over, if anything. I hate to impose on you like this, but how was I to know that there would be a last minute offer from Bloomington, for the same afternoon and for three times the fee? Good luck, and much affection,

Signed Wayne.

Now most of us here have just performed a fantastically intricate intellectual dance together. Without knowing each other, total strangers, we somehow managed to work together in mental patterns so complex that they would certainly baffle the best computer yet devised; indeed I feel quite confident that no one will ever devise a computer capable of doing what we just did. Recently one of our professors of Russian at The University of Chicago received a piece of machine translation to be checked for errors; she works as a consultant to a group trying to develop effective machine translation of scholarly articles—the kind of writing which comes closest to being programmable. Since the article was about economics, she was puzzled to find the frequently repeated phrase "according to the poet." Every few sentences the seemingly sober computer had a kind of emotional breakdown and threw in "according to the poet." It took her awhile to figure out that the poor machine was doing its literal best with the letters which in Russian begin the word meaning "therefore." To human readers the same letters do both jobs very well, because without even taking thought we can receive from the context whatever clues are required to avoid talking about poets when all that is intended is a logical transition.

Clearly you and I performed just now a much more difficult task than was given to that machine. I made a sequence of claims with my words, and my total verbal context supported those words. Yet you were able to translate what I said into meanings entirely different—not "opposite" or "contrary," as some mistaken definitions of irony would say—but variously shaded from near agreement with "the words" to total rejection. I did not wink or nudge or hold up four fingers to indicate quotation marks, and yet you "dug me," as we say. How did you possibly manage to do it?

Well, perhaps we should begin with the honest confession that some of you did not, at least for awhile. Some of you were at first puzzled about why others were so sure so early that something funny was going on. In fact, I judge from the initial dismayed silence that most of you were taken in for a moment or two—at least I hope so. And we can be pretty sure that without the communal clues of the laughter, some of you—I won't try to find out which ones—would have remained deceived right on through to the end of the letter.

Since irony has this power to deceive the unwary, it is often talked about as something designed to deceive some readers and thus make other, shrewder readers feel proud of themselves. I think this view is in part mistaken, but we should begin by admitting just how often irony does get itself misunderstood. You can no doubt think of many examples from your own experience. One that I am especially fond of was given me by Art Buchwald, the newspaper columnist. Suspecting that he must often be misunderstood, I wrote him asking whether he ever received angry letters denouncing him for positions that he had in fact made fun of. He wrote back to say that almost every column produces a good number of such denunciations, and he sent me a small collection that had been written against one column that had been headed "Art Says a Kind Word for Unwed Fathers." Mr. Buchwald had begun the column like this:

> With all the bad news going on throughout the world, there's been one ray of hope recently—emanating from, of all places, England. A welfare council in Essex has announced that it has set up an agency to help unmarried fathers.
>
> Roy Demery, who was appointed by the Moral Welfare Council of Essex, was quoted as saying:
>
> "Unmarried fathers must be helped, not neglected and looked down on. The fact that a girl is having his baby obviously weights heavily on many a man, especially if he is not in the position to marry her. . . . Often he is bullied into wedding her by angry parents. This should not happen if the couple don't love each other."
>
> We hope that the Essex experiment is a success and that a similar program will soon be adopted in this country. The problems of unwed fathers have been ignored by everyone in the United States, while all the attention has been concentrated on the unwed mother. And yet for every unwed mother there is an unwed father somewhere—alone, friendless and needing sympathy.
>
> There are an estimated 3,000 homes in the United States where an unwed mother can apply for help, but there is not one place where an unwed father can seek consolation.
>
> Having spent four years in the U.S. Marines, three years at the University of Southern California and 14 years in Paris, we have always been concerned with the plight of the unmarried father.

And so on. The response of some correspondents to such "obvious" joshing was angry indeed. "Sure do not agree with the man who wrote this article, if it is his opinion, then he must need some kind of 'psychiatric care.' Talk about being a 'man's world,' it sure is." "What is the world coming to, where such things are even *allowed* to be published. . . . If this new idea of yours is going to come under United Fund, we're quitting." This one was signed, "Indignant mother of 1 daughter and 2 lovely granddaughters." "Your column was disgusting. What fathers suffer is infinitesimal to what a girl has to suffer—are you trying to urge them to be more like animals?"

And on they went. One or two letters showed signs of suspicion.

An especially angry one ended, light suddenly dawning: "Or was your column written to give the people a good laugh today?" But it is important to note, as we try to understand what a dangerous weapon Mr. Buchwald had used, that even two letter writers who fully recognized that he was joking were angry with him for joking about such a serious matter!

The history of literature, like the history of everyday life, is strewn with such misunderstandings and denunciations. Many of you know about Defoe's *The Shortest Way with the Dissenters.* Defoe tried to satirize the Tory position of religious dissent by writing a mock argument, ostensibly written by an extreme Tory, about the various kinds of gruesome punishment that ought to be meted out to all dissenters. Many readers took it "straight," and when the hoax was revealed Defoe ended in the stocks for it. An example closer to home was the recent *Report from Iron Mountain* (1967). It purported to be a literal account of a secret summit meeting— business magnates, five-star generals, think-tank directors, powerful politicians—troubled by the problems of what the nation should do in the unpleasant event that peace should break out. It was taken seriously, and generally denounced by reviewers all over the world; even *Punch*, that British journal that commits so many brilliant ironies in its own right, took the report as a serious sign of just how low the Americans had fallen.

You will have noticed that I talk of such readings as mistakes, not as rich and fruitful discoveries of seven new types of ambiguity. In contrast to one critical fashion that seems to say "the more variant readings the better," I want to suggest that at least in this one kind of statement, whether spoken or literary, there is such a thing as a flatly mistaken reading. Obviously such a position is possible only about some of the works that are called ironic, not all. *Irony* is one of the loosest of all critical terms, and to talk sense about any one kind requires that we do some defining. Most of my examples today will be of one quite precise kind, what I shall call "stable irony." All the other kinds we must put to one side, for now, though some of them are in some ways even more interesting: ironies of event—the avalanche that destroys the rescue team, the accidental prediction of disaster, the car driver killed while struggling with his seat belt; unconscious ironies—the speaker who boasts of his humility, the "straight" author whose works fall into the hands of readers who see irony everywhere; and finally "unstable ironies"—the kind of thing offered by many modern ironists who deliberately refuse to allow us any secure grounds for interpretation.

Rather than attempting a formal conceptual definition, let me simply offer four "marks" of stable irony. First, like many other kinds, stable irony is *intended* to be seen as ironic—the speaker expects all or most of his auditors to get the point. Second, unlike many ironic statements, stable ironies are not overt—"Isn't it ironic that . . ."—but *covert*, disguised, sufficiently secret to allow a strong possibility for some readers to go astray. But third, they *are* stable, in the sense that once we have reconstructed a solid platform out of the unstable surface meanings, we have a right to feel some confidence that the author shares our new position. I really *am* Wayne Booth, and there is no one here who feels the slightest doubt about it. Perhaps I need not remind you that there are some ironists who do not think that any stable platform of this kind can ever be found; all ironies for them can be undercut with further ironies. Fourth, it follows from this third mark that stable ironies are in some sense local or finite.

Kierkegaard said that the spirit of irony always will finally undermine everything. It multiplies instabilities until it becomes "absolute infinite negativity." Anyone who wants to make his way through the world without intellectual or practical disaster must learn to deal with "infinite" ironists, too—Samuel Beckett, say, or Donald Barthelme. But for today I shall wrestle only with that less savage beast, the irony that is intended but covert, stable in interpretation and to some degree localized in its reference.

I want to ask two questions about it, first, how we manage to understand it, when there's nobody around to nudge us, and second, why—since it leads so many people astray—*why* does everybody go on using it? You'd think that such a dangerous weapon would have a law passed against it, but instead we find it everywhere, in popular songs ("You don't thrill me when you hold me, no, not much"), in advertisements, in nine out of ten TV programs—in just about everything but the obituary column.

The answers I've been coming to are more complicated, I'm afraid, than I ever dreamed they would be when I began. I've just completed a book of nearly 300 pages on the subject. Of course, a lot of those pages are filled with trash. The trouble is, I don't know which ones yet. In any case, you can be sure that I've picked out the worst ones for today, because I happen to know that there are a lot of idea-thieves in the Purdue English department and I don't want to lose any of my *good* stuff to them.

Now, most of you recognized that I didn't mean that. But *how* did you know? Let's trace the complicated steps you had to take to decide—though you did it "in a flash"—that I could not mean what the words actually said, either just now or in my introduction.

First, you had to decide that there was something wrong, something unacceptable, in what the words seemed to say. You saw that *you* would not have said what I said, in these circumstances, and you would not expect any normal person to say them and mean them.

Second, you had to invent some hypotheses about what was going on when I said something that you thought foolish or arrogant or misinformed, like "Don Browks." One possibility is that I was foolish or ignorant enough to say it and mean it. Another is that you didn't hear me straight. A third is that I was lying and intending you to take it at face value. A fourth is that I was using stable irony, intending an ironic introduction to this lecture on irony.

The third step, more or less simultaneous, was a decision about *me*, to help you choose from among your hypotheses. By now you have a large cluster of beliefs about me, some of them pretty firm, some of them tentative; the cluster—or to be fashionable, the *structure*— has been getting more and more complicated throughout this period. And you found that the picture you had built up did not allow for me to be *quite* stupid enough to say, "I'm giving you my poor stuff and saving the good stuff for my book." No doubt you've heard some pretty awful things from this platform, but no speaker has ever been quite *that* careless. So you decided that I must have been kidding.

Fourth, you had to reconstruct what my real meaning was, with nothing but *your* hunches about *my* hunches about *your* hunches to go on. And somehow you managed to arrive at something like this: "He's really saying something entirely different from what he means, because he really means that he's doing the best he can, poor man, though it may not be good enough even so." Meanwhile I, too, have been relying in rather dangerous ways on my hunches about you. Just think of how disastrous it would have been if you had not laughed at my introduction! Yet I was able to assume that *you* would be the kind of people who would enjoy *my* assumption that *you* would see that *I* could not be the kind of person—and so on. Ad infinitum? No, it is obviously *not* ad infinitum, and that is part of what makes it all so interesting.

I started out, about ten years ago, trying to write a little handbook that would help people take these four steps with confidence, though I hadn't even formulated the steps at that time. Now I no longer believe that such a handbook is possible. The art of reading irony depends on funds of experience with books and with life that I have not been able to codify. Even the experts often go astray, or at least they often disagree with each other, which suggests that one expert or another must have gone astray. And yet we often manage to meet each other with great precision through irony.

Even now I can't explain fully how we do it, but it is easy to make a list of some of the ways that authors *help* us do it. Though there are some modern authors who claim that it is sort of dishonest to give any special help to readers, most authors provide as much help as we should need, if we are willing to keep awake and use whatever is offered. The trouble is, of course, that too many of us too much of the time go through our verbal experiences half asleep. I could happily develop that point, but I wasn't invited here to preach at you—so I'll leave it to you to work up the moral of all this for yourselves.

Let's turn, then, to some of the ways authors have of nudging us into suspecting irony.

The first method is by direct warnings. Sometimes we find direct assertions that we should "watch out," given in a tone of voice that seems unequivocally nonironic. Titles are often a giveaway, like my title for this lecture today. When Thomas Mann called one novel *Felix Krull, Confidence Man*, he surely must have felt that he had given ample warning not to believe anything said by con-man Felix Krull as he tells his own story. Erasmus calls his book *Praise of Folly*; Pope calls his poem *The Dunciad*.

Sometimes an author will save his warning for an epigraph, or he may give it in some kind of preface or statement outside the work. When Nabokov wrote *Lolita*, he knew that some readers would be naive enough to identify his point of view with that of his narrator, Humbert Humbert, so he wrote a postscript saying that Humbert "is a foreigner and an anarchist, and there are many things, besides his [love of] nymphets [like Lolita] in which I disagree with him." Needless to say, the warning was often overlooked by reviewers.

How could they do so? We could assume that they were all plain careless, but I think it is much more complicated than that. There is a special problem about such direct warnings: they *could* also be ironic. How do I know that Nabokov was not being ironic in his postscript, simply to protect himself from an identification with Humbert that would be factually justified. Kenneth Burke once wrote a novel called *Towards a Better Life*, and he has spent some energy since explaining that the title was ironic—his hero does not really move towards a better life. But how do we know whether to believe Burke when he says *that*? Which gets us right back where we started.

The second most obvious kind of clue is the open proclamation of plain error. "Animals talk to each other, of course," Mark Twain began one story. "There can be no question about that; but I suppose there are very few people who can understand them. I never knew but one man who could. I knew he could, however, because he told me so himself" ("Baker's Bluejay Yarn"). Mark Twain knew that you would know that he knew that his speaker is talking nonsense here. But this dramatizes again the circularity of such clues: it's no good for us to decide that what somebody says is a mistake; we must have reason to believe that the real author agrees with us and is therefore setting up the false voice for ironic effect.

Another novel by Nabokov, *Ada*, begins like this: "All happy families are more or less dissimilar; all unhappy ones are more or less alike, says a great Russian writer in the beginning of a famous novel (*Anna Arkadievitch Karenina*, transfigured into English by R. C. Stonelower, Mount Tabor Ltd., 1880)." The reference is specific and it is grossly garbled: the title is wrong, the date is wrong, the translator is wrong, and the opening by Tolstoy says exactly the opposite of the quotation Nabokov gives. As if to offer a special bonus to those who look closely, Nabokov gives a masculine ending to Anna's otherwise fake middle name. Of course one knows all these things only if one knows them—though as one of Thurber's characters always says, "You could look it up." But even if we recognize the errors, how do we decide that Nabokov himself really knows that he's got it wrong? The inferences are complicated here, as always, but they are so easy that nobody has ever doubted the results. The odds against believing that Nabokov, the sophisticated Russian emigré, could be ignorant of his own errors here are so high that I would comfortably bet my income for the remainder of my life on the inference—so well do I know the mind of that stranger, Nabokov, in this world in which some theorists tell us that nobody knows anybody else's mind.

Many authors do not require us to possess the conflicting facts in advance of reading; they offer contradictory facts within the work. Toward the beginning of Pope's *The Rape of the Lock*, we read

> Now lap-dogs give themselves the rousing shake,
> And sleepless lovers, just at twelve, awake.

Well, are the lovers sleepless, or do they awake only at twelve? We can't have it both ways. We can decide, if we don't know Pope very well, that he was just careless with his words here, but those who do know his characteristic irony will expect him to make this kind of jest. Similarly, if we read in Anatole France, "The penguins had the most powerful army in the world. So had the porpoises,"[1] we have assertions of fact that simply cannot be harmonized without assuming either France's stupidity *or* his ironic intention. And the choice is easy for those who know anything about him. Those of you who have studied dramatic irony will know that it usually depends on this kind of clue: a violation by a character later in the play of something we have been shown earlier. "Isn't it wonderful, Hedda," Tesman says in *Hedda Gabler*, "how everything has worked out"—and *we* know how *awful* it is.

The third kind of clue is often discussed as if it were the only kind: it is showing something wrong, or at least unusual, about the speaker's style.

Whenever, in the normal course of perusing a piece of precisely executed writing, whether discursive or imaginative, whether prose or verse, one encounters any radical tergiversation from those perhaps ineluctable norms of expression with which one is accustomed, one should promptly recognize that there is a strong likelihood that ironic obfuscations are being adumbrated.

You notice, I see, what happened to my style in that sentence, and I hope you deplored it. The sudden departure from my usual tone should have alerted you all to an ironic shift. I could have said, moving in the opposite direction, "You gotta watch some writers like a hawk—they'll fool you." When the youthful Jane Austen wrote a mock history of England, she knew how to dissociate herself from her narrator by choosing just the right wrong word: "It was in this reign that Joan of Arc lived and made such a *row* among the English." It is the same effect as when Mark Twain praises a Greek chapel, in *Innocents Abroad*, as "the *showiest* in the Church of the Holy Sepulchre." This is a tough one to apply, since ideas of normal style differ, and when two people disagree about them it is hard to know where to turn for a decisive arbiter.

The fourth kind of clue is even shakier, though we've been relying on it all hour to some degree. Whenever a speaker violates one of your firm beliefs, it may be that the author is agreeing with you behind the speaker's back. "Don't be silly," says a character in a novel by Calder Willingham. "Nobody ever gets raped in the United States. What do you think this is, a barbarous, medieval country?"[2] I have noticed that every student I have known who missed the irony of Swift's modest proposal has condemned the speaker's proposal that children be fattened and killed for meat as a solution to Ireland's economic woes. They all say something like this: "That's a terrible, cruel plan, and anybody who would advance it must be crazy." The next step should have been to ask whether anyone known as a writer would advance such a plan seriously.

So far all we know, really, is how to suspect irony. These clues alert us. What will confirm or deny our suspicion?

I can't go into a full answer today, but I think the question leads us into the whole fascinating problem of how we recognize a literary kind—a genre—when we see one. Because the best final security in deciding whether a word or sentence or paragraph is ironic is knowing the nature of the whole work to which the part contributes. It is true that some sentences give themselves away pretty clearly even out of context. But most could be either straight or ironic, taken in themselves, and only our sense of what sort of literary world we are in can tell us for sure. In grappling with that question, we'll also really be grappling with another hard one, which is how to know when to stop in our ironic interpretation. Too many critics have talked as if the more ironies a reader can see the better, but it should by now be clear that the art of understanding irony is even more a matter of stopping at the right spot than of knowing when to start. (Some of you will have noticed that here and elsewhere today I cheerfully invite you to commit the "intentional fallacy" with me. I simply cannot find any way to discuss how we read ironies without referring to probabilities about the intentions of real authors. Indeed I think that studying ironies requires us to reconsider many modern distinctions between what is "intrinsic" to the work and what is "extrinsic." But for today we must postpone all such encounters with critical controversy.)

We have, then, direct warnings; implied warnings in factual error, either conflicting with facts in the world outside the work or given in it; and conflicts of belief. Each of these four tests is extremely fallible, but they are all we have to go on, in looking for what we might call advance clues, as distinct from the tests we can apply once we have a chance to take in an entire work and study how its parts interrelate.

I'm going now to read you a complete work, a short one but complete. It appeared all by itself, as it were, with no author's signature, in a magazine. How much difficulty do you have, if any, in deciding whether the word "delighted," which occurs at the beginning, is intended ironically?

Censorship

We are delighted with the recent censorship ruling in the matter of motion-picture harems. Some scenes in a Paramount picture now in production are set in a harem, and after careful deliberation the censors have decided to allow this type of polyform allure *provided* the boudoir does not contain the sultan. The girls can mill about among the pillows, back and side having gone bare, but no male eye must gaze upon them—save, of course, yours, lucky reader. This harem-but-no-sultan decision belongs in the truly great body of opinion interpreting the American moral law. It takes its place alongside the celebrated 1939 ruling on the exposure of female breasts in the Flushing World of Tomorrow, which provided that one breast could be presented publicly but not two, and thereby satisfied the two seemingly irreconcilable groups: the art-lovers, who demanded breasts but were willing to admit that if you'd seen one you'd seen them both, and the decency clique, who held out for concealment but were agreed that the fact of concealing one breast established the essential reticence of the owner and thereby covered the whole situation, or chest. That subtle and far-reaching ruling carried the Fair, as we know, safely through two difficult seasons, and we imagine that the aseptic harem will do as much for Hollywood.[3]

If anyone now questioned our claim that E. B. White means the word "delighted" in a very special, largely negative sense in that opening statement, and means the phrase "truly great" to mean something like "truly ridiculous," we would feel great confidence that he was wrong. Once we have experienced a literary work as a given, recognizable kind of thing, we are told by it, as it were, what to do with every word in it. In this case we all experienced a piece of satire, using pretended praise as blame, and it *placed* the irony for us decisively; we know that it would be as absurd to think that White does not intend irony as to think that he intended us to go further. Nobody could ever make the mistake, for example, of saying that the piece suggests an ironic undercutting for itself, with White really showing himself as a censor censoring the censors. *We* know that the *author* knew that *we* would know that the *author* must have intended *us* to recognize that *he* would never have doubted that *we* would know precisely that *he* . . .

The miracle we are grappling with is that such a chain of inferences does not move to an infinite regress. We know, sometimes, where to stop, and in doing so we know something about the second question I have raised. Why use irony, anyway, when it gives so much trouble by causing frequent misunderstanding? I have time today only to touch on the answer.

If you think back over our many examples and ask what happened to those readers who understood the irony, you'll already see something of the answer to our Why question. First, while all those baffled readers of Buchwald were spouting their angry charges, Buchwald was reaping the profits of a very close partnership with the other readers who were not baffled. The very intricacy of our interpretative act builds for us, when we manage to do it right, a tight bond with the author: to understand him, we've had to assume that he is our kind of person, and that he knows that we will know that he knows that we will assume—etc. The result is that most literary effects that will allow for stable irony at all will be strengthened by it. Even though some readers or listeners may be left by the wayside, those who come along will be clamped inescapably into the author's patterns—they will in fact have the illusion of having built each point for themselves.

A suggestion of how powerful this effect can be is found in something Edith Wharton said about her friendship with Henry James:

> The real marriage of true minds is for any two people to possess a sense of humour or irony pitched in exactly the same key, so that their joint glances at any subject cross like interarching search-lights. I have had good friends between whom and myself that bond was lacking, but they were never really intimate friends; and in that sense Henry James was perhaps the most intimate friend I ever had, though in many ways we were so different.[4]

I have time now at the end only to touch briefly on two other values realized by stable irony—when it works. First, it is an almost incredibly economical form of communication. If we try to "unpack" what is said in even the simplest ironies, we find ourselves with at least two or three times as many words as there are in the original statement. And even then we have captured only the more inert portion of the "message." The active engagement of two human beings, one inviting to an elaborately formal dance of the mind, the other accepting the invitation and entitled to take pride in his own performance—none of this "performative" aspect can be translated into nonironic words. When Samuel Butler leads his narrator in *Erewhon* to near disaster and then has him say ". . . As luck would have it, providence was on my side," the sheer quantity of "secret" communication between Butler and any reader who gets his joke is immense. If in describing it "straight" I try to include some account of the cultural preconceptions on which the silent communion depends, I find that I need two to three hundred words at a minimum, and even then, of course, the emotional force has been dissipated.

No doubt this splendid economy contributes to a third value— the implication in most stable irony that the speaker has a kind of wisdom about life that nobody who always speaks in literal sobriety possesses. "We" are the insiders, we know what we know, we have seen the wheels within wheels that make this complex and mysterious world go round. I, the ironist, appeal to your desire for profundities—though neither of us may be able to state quite what they are. The universe seems, in our laconic but intricate discourse about even the simplest thing in it, a richer, more mysterious thing than it can ever seem when our words mean only what they "say." No wonder, then, that once ironists and their readers have learned to savor the delights of obliquity, they soon learn to multiply them, and then to multiply further—until suddenly they are dealing no longer with what can be called *stable* irony at all. What began as a secure but secret dance together becomes an encounter with increasing instabilities. Whatever platform I try out, in attempting my interpretations, is pulled out from under me by some further irony, and before I know it the ironist and I are whirling dizzily toward chaos.

I hate to leave you in such a state, and I wish that there were time today to take a cool look at some of the unstable ironists of recent decades. In the book I am just completing on irony, I use as my main example Samuel Beckett. But you have no doubt encountered many like him in your literature courses, and you probably have no need for one more demonstration of just how disorienting such ironies can be.

So many modern authors have indulged in the heady delights of instability that talk about irony has generally treated it as the mother of confusion, or as an elitist protection from reality or commitment, or as an expression of man's isolation in an absurd universe. It can be all those things, but I have chosen today to look lovingly at how irony can become the source of some of life's most intimate and rewarding and unbreakable friendships. Art Buchwald and E. B. White and the many great ironists I have not even mentioned—such as Fielding, or E. M. Forster, to say nothing of classical figures like Lucian or Continental masters like Voltaire—all of them convince us that we are brothers and sisters under the skin—the surface that is only a set of hints about what they really offer us.

I think that in studying carefully how the same figure of speech can give rise to such conflicting responses, to the tightest of bondings and the most exasperating confusions, to high praise and to total condemnation, we learn something of how even our everyday nonironic communication works. In doing so we always labor under the ironic gaze of Supreme Irony, the God of that Truth which Socrates tried to teach us: nobody ever learns very much about anything. But at the same time we do learn *something* of how to make our way in the whole mysterious world of symbolic exchange.

Rhetoric, Poetics, and Philosophy

Kenneth Burke

Just as I was trying to decide how I should begin this talk, I came upon Harold Toliver's interesting volume, *Animate Illusions: Explorations of Narrative Structure*,[1] where he devotes some pages to Vaihinger, Burke, and Stevens in a section entitled "Pragmatic Views of 'As If.'" He begins the section with a quotation from Vaihinger's book, *The Philosophy of "As If."* And I in turn shall quote it:

> The treatment of ideational forms of the whole conceptual world as mere products of the imaginative faculty was originally accomplished by Hume and Kant, and continued by Schopenhauer and Herbart. But to treat them as fictions in our sense is to include the idea that these constructions are, from a logical point of view, identical with scientific fictions, i.e., with constructs that, from a practical point of view, are useful and necessary, though theoretically they are false (p. 37).

It so happened that, in a class at the University of Pittsburgh, we had been concentrating for a time on the subject of metaphor, using in particular three books: I. A. Richards's *The Philosophy of Rhetoric*, Colin Murray Turbayne's *The Myth of Metaphor*, and my *Permanence and Change* (which I had originally called *Treatise on Communication* and which has the subtitle *An Anatomy of Purpose*).[2] Though Turbayne frequently uses the formula "as if" (which Vaihinger developed from Kant), he makes no mention of Vaihinger. Richards mentions Vaihinger in connection with Bentham's "theory of Fictions." Burke knew Bentham but not Vaihinger at the time when he wrote *Permanence and Change*—but in general he put his stress upon metaphor and analogy (terms generally treated as synonymous, frequently a quite justified procedure which both Richards and Turbayne also exemplify).

The point of all this is my involvement in an attempt to ask how metaphor (analogy, "as if") taken as starting-point, can help guide us (if it can!) through the intricacies of our subject, "Rhetoric, Poetics, Philosophy." And to what extent can we be talking literally, even though there is a sense in which everything we say is either a live metaphor or a dead one? And that you may see where we are going, or trying to go, let me say at the start: the speaker appears before you as an advocate with an investment to protect. He has a theory which he would dignify by classification as an "ism," yet he himself in some of his earlier writings was guilty of contributing to the very usage that he would now find fault with. I have in mind references to the "Dramatistic *metaphor*." But I shall try to uphold the proposition that Dramatism is *literal*. People *do act*. It is metaphorical to call them "machines" which but *move*.

Since you'll be asked to twist and turn a lot in what is to follow, doubtless I should begin by asking you to get one point "perfectly clear." With regard to poetics, though truth may often contribute to a work's appeal, I take it that some variant of what in the old days was called "verisimilitude" is the basic active principle, which is in turn interwoven with the work's ways of unfolding, that is, its *form*.

Similarly, with regard to rhetoric, I take it that not truth but opinion is the surest ground of persuasion—and Aristotle seems to have implied considerations of that sort when distinguishing between enthymeme and syllogism. Often, though not always, truth helps—yet many questions are called "rhetorical" precisely because there is no "truth" to which one can refer. For instance with the kind of rhetorical induction that is got, in deliberative oratory, by the application of some example from the past to a hypothetical outcome of the future, it must be a matter of opinion as to whether the similarities between the two cases are greater than their differences (since obviously the two cases will be far from identical). At the same time, we must not think of opinion and truth as necessarily at odds, since many opinions can be quite sound.

But to our texts. I offer two excuses for beginning with my own book. Besides being the first of the three to appear, it affords me the best opportunity to set things up in ways handiest for my concern with the qualifications needed for considering the affinities and allies of Dramatism as a *philosophy*. For my discussion of philosophy must center in my concern with the role of "symbolic action" in philosophy. In the widest sense, things line up thus: Viewing our subject in terms of "symbolic action," we treat poetics as concerned with "symbolic action" in and for itself, rhetoric as concerned with the role of "symbolic action" in persuasion and identification, science as the use of "symbolic action" to the ends of factual knowledge, and philosophy as the use of "symbolic action" for the discussion of first principles. There are other considerations, but these should suffice for present purposes. The cluster of concerns that center about metaphor and are revealed by our perhaps somewhat vexing attempt to consider the lot may be as good a way as any of lining things up. I shall start by putting together some passages from *Permanence and Change*.

"Though we usually think of abstraction as a very subtle process, from another point of view it may be considered a very blunt one. The scales abstract, for instance, when their dial registers their inability to distinguish a pound of feathers from a pound of lead. They judge by excluding all but their definitions of weight" (p. 57). "Our senses themselves are similar abstracters, abstracting or interpreting certain events as having a sound-character, a taste-character, a heat-character, a sight-character, etc." (This is what Richards has in mind, I believe, when he refers to a "primordial abstractness" [*The Philosophy of Rhetoric*, p. 36].) For as Helmholtz pointed out, "our very sensory equipment is a set of recording instruments that turn certain events into a certain kind of sign, and we find our way through life on the basis of these signs" (p. 106). "Any living genus possesses an authority of its own, since different genera manifest totally different 'laws' of growth and action. As M. H. Woodger observes in his *Biological Principles*, whereas the doctrine of evolution is based upon a theory of continuity, assuming the uniform and constant operation of natural law, its own theory of 'mutations' directly violates this belief in the constancy of natural law. For when a new race of organisms arises, a new set of 'laws' arises. Let a new kind of grasshopper come into being, for instance, and you have a new set of 'principles', which move certain bits of the universe about in certain ways. Conversely, were this family of grasshopper completely destroyed, certain 'laws' of movement would have passed out of the universe" (p. 232).

I here began a bit off from center, but it's a handy way of approaching metaphor via a concern with the "interrelation of Analogy, Metaphor, Abstraction, Classification, Interest, Expectancy, and Intention" (p. 103). That is to say: any abstraction, be it verbal or sensory, *classifies*. It involves interests in a physiological sense, insofar as one kind of organism is motivated by a class of risks and desideranda ("expectations" and "intentions") peculiar to its species and situation. When such classification is conceptual, as with the difference, say, between the abstractions (or generalized categories) of physics and psychoanalysis, classifications fall across one another on the bias. Abstraction and classification and expectation and intention are obviously all involved in such a statement as "I shall gather some wood, to build a fire," though one cannot foresee the exact details of one's operation, quite as one cannot exactly foresee the details of an automobile trip organized in accordance with the abstractions of a road map that gives him some rudimentary instructions about the route.

"Analogy" figures in the sense that the references to building a fire in the future involve an analogy of some sort with previous contexts in which some such content as fire or fire-making figured. In certain respects, this new "intended" event would be "analogous" to some previous event already experienced. Even if I had never actually collected wood for a fire before, I'd be referring to something in some way "analogous."

But what of "metaphor"? Beyond all question, if I had said, "I'm going to build a fire under that guy," you'd distinguish immediately between *literal* and *metaphorical* meanings of my sentence. And there our problem comes to a focus, with the help of a quotation from one of the most ingenious books I ever read, *The Misuse of Mind*, by Karin Stephen, (New York: Harcourt, Brace, 1922). "In order to get around the almost universal tendency to confuse abstractions with facts," she writes:

> Bergson sometimes tries to get us to see the facts as they actually are by using metaphor instead of description in terms of abstract general notions. He has been much criticised for this but there is really a good deal to be said for attempting to convey facts by substituting metaphors for them rather than by using the ordinary intellectual method of substituting abstractions reached by analysis. Those who have criticised the use of metaphor have for the most part not realized how little removed such description is from the ordinary intellectual method of analysis. They have supposed that in analysis we stick to the fact itself, whereas in using metaphor we substitute for the fact to be described some quite different fact which is only connected with it by a more or less remote analogy. If Bergson's view of the intellectual method is right, when we describe in abstract terms we are not sticking to the facts at all, we are substituting something else for them just as much as if we were using an out and out metaphor. Qualities and all abstract general notions are, indeed, nothing but marks of analogies between a given fact and all the other facts belonging to the same class: they may mark rather closer analogies than those brought out by an ordinary metaphor, but on the other hand in a frank metaphor we at least stick to the concrete, we substitute fact for fact and we are in no danger of confusing the fact introduced by the metaphor with the actual fact to which the metaphor applies (pp. 94-95; in Stephen's book, pp. 58-59).

To which I added, "Indeed, as the documents of science pile up, are we not coming to see that whole works of scientific research, even entire *schools*, are hardly more than the patient repetition, in all its ramifications, of a fertile metaphor?[3] . . . The attempt to fix argument by analogy as a distinct kind of process, separable from logical argument, seems increasingly futile. The most practical form of thought that one can think of, the invention of some new usable device, has been described as analogical extension, as when one makes a new machine by conceiving of some old process, such as the treadle, the shuttle, the wheel, the see-saw, the wedge, etc., carried over into some set of facts to which no one had previously felt that it belonged" (pp. 95-96).

"Carried over" is itself as etymologically strict a translation as you could get of the Greek word, "metaphor." But I do wish I could remember where I had picked up the term, "analogical extension"; for (as both Richards's and Turbayne's books make apparent) *there* is the strategic term for both metaphor and analogy.

In the summarizing section of *Permanence and Change* (pp. 255-61), I worked with a corrective concept of "recalcitrance" whereby a metaphorical statement such as "I can safely jump from this high place" might be revised to "I can safely jump from this high place with the aid of a parachute." For "the universe 'yields' to our point of view by disclosing the different orders of recalcitrance which arise when the universe is considered from this point of view" (p. 257).

Also, I had hit upon a parting of the ways between metaphorical extension and analogical extension (a distinction that often is not necessary), when investing in an analogical extension that got me to metaphor by a quite different route. For, having decided to define piety (along lines suggested by Santayana), as "loyalty to the sources of our being," I so "extended" the principle "analogically" that the members of the gashouse gang could be called in their peculiar way "pious," as a mentally disturbed person might be in his (since he devoutly brought fitting gifts to the altar of his distress). And by that route I came upon the concept of "perspective by incongruity," a mode of analogical extension got by combining terms that one usually thought of as at odds with each other. (Only a deliberate "perspective by incongruity" would see in the gashouse gang's cult of the vulgar a kind of "piety.")

But though I still abide by the book, there's one major point I would no longer go along with. I refer to the title of the culminating section, "The Poetry of Action." I would now make a flat distinction between the practical act of getting in out of the rain and the purely symbolic act of writing a poem about getting in out of the rain. The one is literal, the other figurative, topical, metaphorical. Yet hold, alas! To say as much is eventually to come upon ways whereby they get mixed up all over again. We shall revert to that point later.

2

As regards rhetoric, poetic, and philosophy, all three, a major resource of language is its reliance upon *classification* of some sort. Both Richards and Turbayne favor the word "sorting." Richards points out (p. 36) that such a classificatory process *begins* in "recurrences of like behaviors"; for behind "a particular impression" there has been "a coming together of sortings." That is, any particular object would be a convergence of many attributes each of which could be classed otherwise, as a watch could be classed with round things, solid things, sometimes with ticking things, etc.

Turbayne similarly views metaphor as a kind of "sort-crossing" (along with "make-believe," an "as if" element). A metaphor becomes a "myth" if we use it without "awareness," his word for the kind of discount I had in mind when referring to "recalcitrance." If we use a metaphor without making allowance for (without being "aware" of) its metaphorical quality, it can even become the generating principle of a metaphysics, like the Cartesian view of man as a sort of machine with a soul (p. 62).

However clear the difference between a literal statement like "both lions and men are animals" and a metaphorical one like "he is lion-hearted," the issue readily becomes confused. Etymologically, to call a human being a "person" is to use a metaphor, quite as we are extending a metaphor if we call a human being a "machine." The problem I ultimately confront in this talk is that I would view the personalist perspective as literal, and the mechanistic one as metaphorical; but the confirmed behaviorist would avow that he is doing precisely the opposite, though I shall argue that he is not really (actually, literally) doing what he says he is. Meanwhile quite as my concerns with classification and conflicting ways of classifying got me into speaking sometimes of "analogical extension" and sometimes of "metaphorical extension," so Richards's concern with sorting sometimes involves the term "analogy," while the last two of the six lectures are concerned specifically with "metaphor." And Turbayne's book on sorting and cross-sorting advertises "metaphor" in its title, while frequently using the term "analogy" though it is not listed in his index.

In all three books, the discussion leads quite spontaneously and unnoticeably into the notion of "extension" or "stretching." A good one in Richards's case is in his chapter on "The Command of Metaphor":

> Last time I generalized, or stretched, the sense of the term metaphor—almost you may think to the breaking point. I used it to cover all cases where a word, in Johnson's phrase, "gives us two ideas for one," where we compound different uses of the word into one, and speak of something as though it were another. And I took it further still to include, as metaphoric, those processes in which we perceive or think of or feel about one thing in terms of another—as when looking at a building it seems to have a face and to confront us with a peculiar expression. I want to insist that this sort of thing is normal in full perception and that study of the growth of our perceptions (the animistic world of the child and so on) shows that it must be so (pp. 116-17).

In a sense, analogical or metaphorical extension is the very essence of language. For language is possible only because we can use the same words over and over again; which is to say that we can apply them to many situations. Yet no two situations are identical. As Edward H. Levi states the case in *An Introduction to Legal Reasoning*, (Chicago: University of Chicago Press, 1948):

> . . . The scope of a rule of law, and therefore its meaning, depends upon a determination of what facts will be considered similar to those present when the rule was first announced. The finding of similarity or difference is the key step in the legal process. . . . It is not what the prior judge intended that is of any importance; rather it is what the present judge, attempting to see the law as a fairly consistent whole, thinks should be the determining classification. . . . The problem for the law is: When will it be just to treat different cases as though they were the same? A working legal system must therefore be willing to pick out key similarities and to reason from them to the justice of applying a common classification (pp. 2-3).

The author is here saying in effect that, when basing his decision upon precedent, the judge must ask himself whether the two cases are analogous, for it is obvious that in an almost countless number of details they must differ. Thinking along the same lines, in my *Attitudes Toward History* (New York: New Republic, 1937, pp. 229ff, of revised edition) I proposed the term, "casuistic stretching," to characterize a procedure whereby

> one introduces new principles while theoretically remaining faithful to old principles. . . . The devices for ostensibly retaining allegiance to an "original principle" by casuistic stretching eventually lead to demoralization, which can only be stopped by a new start. . . . All "metaphorical extension" is an aspect of casuistic stretching. . . . Since language owes its very existence to casuistry, casuistic stretching is beyond all possibility of "control by elimination.' . . . In Shakespeare, casuistry was absolute and constant. He could make new "metaphorical extensions" at random. He could leap across the categories of association [Turbayne would call it "sort-crossing, with awareness"] as readily as walking. The mortmain of dead metaphors ("abstractions") that has gripped us since his time has rigidified this original liquidity.

And any such "over-simplification" that is maintained by casuistic stretching "must be corrected in turn by *latitudinarianism*, which is another word for casuistic stretching." And I see that I hook in with Turbayne's term when saying that, since the world is too complex for such simplifications, one can only hope to "take up the slack" by "increased awareness."

The term "analogical extension" is in essence a pleonasm; for analogy by its very nature is a stretching. Logicians point out that it can serve as an ingenious halfway stage between univocal and equivocal terms. For no term that in effect but likens one situation to another can be wholly univocal. And there is a sense in which the application of the same term to two different *things* or *objects* could be viewed similarly, since any individual thing is but part of a wider context that is left unmentioned, an issue which Richards touches upon (p. 34) when noting how words are in effect the "abridgements" of contexts. I get involved in the same issue when on the subject of "contextual definition" (*Grammar of Motives*, pp. 24-26) thus: "Starting from the Aristotelian notion that a substance, or being, is to be considered 'in itself' (*kath auto*, which Spinoza rendered *id quod per se concipitur*), Spinoza went on to observe that nothing less than the *totality of all that exists* can meet this requirement."[4]

3

At the beginning of his book, Richards offers a definition of rhetoric that, while not alien to an Aristotelian position, slights the traditional role Aristotle assigns to "topics" (in the art of persuasion): "Rhetoric, I shall urge, should be a study of misunderstanding and its remedies." And just before his closing quotation from the *Timaeus* he says that his lectures "began by claiming that the study of Rhetoric must, in a certain sense, be philosophical."

Analogical extension, or the establishing of a perspective by the "casuistic stretching" of a metaphor (or of any term, such as the title for some "ism" or other) would seem to be a standard resource of the rhetorical, poetical, and philosophic realms, all three. Where Aristotle views rhetoric and dialectic as "counterparts" of each other, the Stoics inclined to think of dialectic as the philosophical ground of rhetoric. And in the assumptions, or "equations," of either poetic or rhetorical symbol-using there is a philosophy *implied*, though the writer or speaker may not be the person who could make such implications systematically explicit.

In that technical sense at least, the realms of rhetoric and poetic are grounded in philosophy. Yet when watching how often Richards makes his points by turning things around, one feels admonished to try seeing what happens if we proceed by turning the term "the philosophy of rhetoric" into the term "the rhetoric of philosophy."

My deceased friend, Bob Coates, told me that he had experimented with such reversals for many years—but by far the best result he got was: "You can lead a horse to drink, but you can't make him water." My favorite that I'm forever citing is Veblin's "Invention is the mother of necessity." Richards's book has many good examples of such reversal. For instance, consider his remarks about the primordial generality and abstractness of meaning and about how, when we mean the simplest-seeming concrete object, its concreteness comes to it from the way in which we are bringing it simultaneously into a number of sorts. The sorts grow together in it to form that meaning. Theory here, as so often, can merely exploit the etymological hint given in the word "concrete" (pp. 35-36).

If we forget this and suppose that we start with discrete impressions of particulars ("fixities and definites" as Coleridge called them) and then build these up into congeries, the theorem I am recommending collapses at once into contradictions and absurdities. That was the fault of the old Hartleian Associationism. . . . It did not go back far enough, it took particular impressions as its initial terms. But the initial terms for this theorem are not impressions; they are sortings, recognitions, laws of response, recurrence of like behaviors (p. 36).

I believe that stress upon language as a way into thoughts about reality often involves such reversals by a change of starting point. My *Rhetoric of Religion*, for instance, confronts the thought that whereas orthodox ontology might say "because we have free will we can act," logology would turn things around, saying instead: "Implicit in the idea of an act there is the idea of freedom, along with, of course, corresponding ideas of bondage."

A formula such as the "rhetoric of philosophy" would involve such considerations as what, in my *Grammar of Motives*, I call the "scene-act ratio," by which I mean that our interpretation of an act is a function of the scene in which we think of it as enacted. It's one kind of act, that is, if it's thought of as enacted against a polytheistic background, with quarrels among the gods making us as though a battlefield trampled upon by opposing supernatural forces. It's a different sort of act if thought of with relation to one God. It's still different if placed in terms of a godless Darwinian setting, or more locally in terms of capitalism, and so on. Any such philosophical circumference is rhetorically persuasive insofar as it ultimately implies what corresponding attitudes would be reasonable and what modes of conduct would be possible. And by the same token, imaginings that are related in one way or another to the contents of narrative, drama, the lyric and the like would implicitly or explicitly tie the implicit philosophy in with the realm of poetics.

In *Permanence and Change* (p. 89, for instance) I classified metaphor as a kind of "perspective" (in the sense that, by putting together terms from different categories of association, it gives us an insight not germane to either such category when taken alone). For instance, Spengler's concept of the "contemporaneous" as applying not simply to things that coexisted at the same time in history but to things existing in analogous stages of different cultures, "makes it possible for him to speak, let us say, of Arabian Puritanism, thus extending the use of a term [there is our word "extending" again] by taking it from the content in which it was habitually used and applying it to another." Thus, "we can discuss the Pergamene quality in Wagner, the Mozartian elements in Phidias, the calculus mathematics emergent in Gothic," etc. And I can make the point for our purposes regardless of how sympathetic or unsympathetic may be our views on Spengler: "These are historical perspectives, which Spengler acquires by taking a word usually applied to one setting and transfering its use to another setting" (p. 90).

I propose to call any such usage a "perspective by incongruity" since the author established any such transference "by violating the 'properties' of the word in its previous linkages." And as I explain in my text, I got to that formula, "perspective by incongruity," a bit roundabout. For I had been struck by Nietzsche's use of the term, "perspective." And when looking back at it in the light of Spengler's tricks for *extending* the concept of the contemporaneous, I realized that the stylistic trick in Nietzsche's "perspectives" at their best was due to the ways of diction whereby that half-madman half-genius did cut across the categories of "what goes with what." Here's one set of what-goes-with-what's; there's another set of what-goes-with-what's; the two associational sets are disrelated until the style of a half-madman half-genius leaps across the gap like a lightning flash, thereby joining them, in what I would call a "perspective by incongruity."

Later, in trying to decide just what is the exact difference between a metaphor and a "perspective by incongruity," I guess it's but a matter of degree. To be sure, when on the subject of *Models and Metaphor: Studies in Language and Philosophy*, Max Black's[5] "'interaction' view of metaphor" and the "extensions of meaning" involved (p. 42) build around the notion that a metaphor has "two distinct subjects" which are "often best regarded as 'systems of things' rather than 'things.'" And "the metaphor works by applying to the principal subject a system of 'associated implications' characteristic of the subsidiary subject" (p. 44).

But though I am not quite sure how I might best distinguish between metaphor in its simplicity and that hybridizing of categories I called "perspective by incongruity," in its most radical manifestation a "perspective by incongruity" comes close to being the *wholly rational* equivalent of an oxymoron, which in my dictionary is defined as "figure of speech with pointed conjunction of seeming contradictories (e.g., *faith unfaithful kept him falsely true*)." But "perspective by incongruity" is not that alone; as some of you may know, my prime examples are Veblen's "trained incapacity" and Eliot's "decadent athleticism." And I explicitly built my next book, *Attitudes Toward History*, around the perspective by incongruity, "bureaucratization of the imaginative," in view of the fact that usually associations clustering around "bureaucratization" are in one realm and associations clustering around "imagination" are in another. In my definition of man, the clause "rotten with perfection" is a perspective by incongruity, perhaps but a perversely figurative way of saying "given to excess."

The realms covered by "analogical extension" and "metaphorical extension" overlap. But much analogical extension is not figurative at all and is not even recognized as involving analogy. Think, for instance, of what wide motivational variations and allegiances are included under such titular terms as Republican or Democrat. And the term "conservative" is stretched to cover many policies that have radically revolutionized and are still radically revolutionizing all mankind's traditional ways of life.

But I still have to try out with you a thesis which even some of you who are not to be included among the Fundamentalists of Behaviorism might incline to question. Though I have found many people who are somewhat charitable toward the Dramatistic perspective as a *metaphor*, I want to see what can be said for it as *literally* grounded.

In keeping with my talk of "reversal," here's how I would apply the principle this time: if the Dramatistic model were but a metaphor extended (the Turbayne view of models), the notion that people act would be but a corollary of that particular "fiction," or "as if," or "make believe." But I would turn things around. Beginning with the proposition, or primal literal intuition, that *persons act*, while things *but move*, I would *derive* the proposition that, in trying to decide what key terms are implicitly to be featured in the idea of an act, one should use a Dramatistic model for heuristic purposes. For the term "act" isn't just sitting out there, all by itself. There's a whole set of terms, clustering around it, as we discover when trying to track down all the key terms implicit in the idea of an "act."

In that sense, my proposition that "persons act, things but move" has the same cards-face-up-on-the-table function as Descartes's "*cogito, ergo sum,*" or Berkeley's "*esse* is *percipi,*" or Spinoza's pantheistic equation, *Deus sive Natura*, or idealism's subject-object pair, or Skinner's ingeniously worrisome reduction to "contingencies of reinforcement." But before pursuing that line further, we should deal with a central aspect of Turbayne's book on the "myth of metaphor."

Turbayne's book explicitly builds about the use of an analogy. Taking some problems that greatly exercised Newton and Descartes in the field of vision, by much ingenious theorizing he offers alternative solutions. To give even a fairly adequate account of his exposition step by step would require more space than all these preceding pages. But fortunately for present purposes I need but

Kenneth Burke

characterize the *principle* involved in his way of attacking the problem. For this quotation helps you see quite readily how he proceeded:

> . . . when we say "I see a watch" or "I see the color, size, shape, etc., of the watch," . . . we need only hold that we have succeeded in finding the meaning of certain visual words: these visual words we call in our metalanguage "white," "small," "round," etc., and their meaning, when they are thus conjoined in our experience, we call "watch." Thus the physical objects that we see in space are meanings that we assign to visual words (p. 134).

His underlying thesis is one that I can subscribe to zestfully. He says that the "metaphor" of mechanism, when used without sufficient "awareness" of its metaphorical aspect, becomes transformed into a "metaphysics of mechanism." And to show that this fusion of sort-crossing is but a confusion, and that "it is only a metaphor" not properly discounted as such, he says:

> . . . the best way to show this is to invent a new metaphor. I therefore treat the events in nature *as if* they compose a language, in the belief that the world may be treated just as well, if not better, by making believe that it is a universal language instead of a giant clockwork (p. 5).

By explicitly applying the term "visual words" to appearances that are not literally words at all, Turbayne would evade the limitations of a model that is presented as literal but is actually an extended metaphor used without proper "awareness" of its metaphorical nature. To this end, by treating our visual impressions as if they were a language that, like the words of a language, involve considerations of *context*, he contrives quite persuasively to offer solutions for certain key problems of vision which in particular exercised Newton and Descartes.

Turbayne's procedure amounts to saying, "Let's think of the things we see (such as the moon looking bigger when near the horizon than when at the zenith) as though such things were 'visual words.' Hence, we'll study their appearances as we would study verbal contexts in which the conjoined words contribute to the interpretation of one another." Regrettably, in this book (though he may have done so elsewhere) he never mentions the astounding exhibits that Adelbert Ames, Jr., set up, to show how our expectations affect our interpretation of what we see. (I refer to such things as the room in which, if A and B but change places, whereas A had looked tall and B short, A now looks short and B tall.) In any case, at least, the all-important matter of *context* figures in both Turbayne's "visual words" and Ames's tricks with perspective and the like.

Both Turbayne and Ames are considering such problems from the standpoint of philosophy, insofar as scientific data about the nature

26

of visual illusion and about the interpretation of visual phenomena may have philosophic implications. But my theories of "identification" in my *Rhetoric of Motives* involve some considerations of rhetoric and poetic that neither Turbayne nor Ames need be concerned with. And a philosophic issue figures, too.

From the standpoint of our subject as a whole, might not Turbayne's resistance to geometrical and mechanistic "metaphors," welcome as it is, be viewed as somewhat victimized by the very position it has gone all-out against? His metaphor of things as "visual words" has the objects of nature in effect communicating such *sheerly naturalistic* messages as "I am round," or "I am farther off than I seem," and the like. For his purposes, there is no reason why he should have done anything more.

But the concept of "identification," as developed in my *Rhetoric of Motives* brings up further considerations, as viewed from this standpoint of rhetoric, poetic, and philosophy in general. It is my claim that, in putting itself against supernaturalism, naturalism becomes over-thorough. For besides the possible anagogic relationship between the realm of nature and the realm of the supernatural, there is the intermediate relationship between the realm of nature (in its sheer physicality) and the realm of the social, the relationship I call the socio-anagogic. Things, as "visual words," are not just saying the kind of things that some naturalists might consider as literal geometric and mechanistic "facts." Things, by reason of their *identification* with aspects of social hierarchy, are saying things like "I am up but you are down," or "I am a threat to the likes of you," or "I stand for the promise of reward," or "Buy me, and you're in." Richards talks about an angle of it in his remarks on the "Club Spirit" (pp. 77-80). Carlyle gives us a lot of it in *Sartor Resartus*. Marx is talking about it in his terms "class consciousness" and "the fetishism of commodities." My most efficient instance is probably in the pages on Henry James's preface to his novel *The Spoils of Poynton*, concerning heirlooms as "household gods" (cf. *A Rhetoric of Motives*, pp. 294-98).

But have I not painted myself into a corner? Let's see. I have said that we begin with the literal proposition, or intuition, "Persons act, things but move." With that as generating principle, I *literally* define man as the symbol-using animal. I *literally* assert that precisely his aptitude for learning arbitrary conventional symbol-systems (such as tribal languages), and his corresponding *need* to learn such, is what constitutes him as a *person* rather than a *thing*. I literally say that such symbolicity is a medium between man and the nonverbal, but by the same token, in being a medium, it separates him from the nonverbal realm (as presumably, say, a worm is not separated from its "reality"). Thus, I literally say that this medium is the source of "symbolic action." Then I *literally* ask, "What is implicit in the idea of an act?" I literally say that, since drama is built about the featuring of "action," I will take drama as a heuristic model that helps me ask what to look for, what to look out for, how, and why. That is to say, I am deriving the choice of model from the term "symbolic action" as my generating principle, which leads me to use the model, not as metaphoric "proof" of anything, but as a heuristic device that helps me clarify what it is to be the typically symbol-using animal. What more literal book than Aristotle's *Rhetoric*? What more literal addition to it than the statement that people become identified with various causes, groups, etc.? And though one might disagree in particular cases, what more literal than the general proposition that, since *natural* things become identified with *social* judgments (as with the distinction between a hovel and a castle), they are not just "visual words" as per Turbayne's metaphor, they embody in all literalness, for man the symbol-using animal, a realm of motivation as obviously literally there as might be the case with the literal choice between hovel and castle.

True, there is a sense in which we cannot so much as speak without using fictions. Or there is a sense in which, as Richards says, (p. 94) *"Thought* is metaphoric, and proceeds by comparison, and the metaphors of language derive therefrom." But if metaphor is all, there must at least be metaphor and metaphor, since I take it that everything Richards says about metaphor is to be understood literally.

In that sense, the "Dramatistic" statement that "persons act" is literal, even though the very word "person" is etymologically derived from a word for "mask," as a figurative word for "role," and might reflect a time when the only "persons" were "parsons," in keeping with a "calling," or vocation.

Addendum

Hopefully, I give myself one last chance.

In sum, the conditions for a human "person" are: (1) a biological organism capable of sensations associated with pleasure and pain and (2) such an organism must be endowed with the aptitude (and the corresponding need) to acquire a conventional symbol-system (such as a tribal language) that has the ability to comment on itself ("self-consciousness").

Such conditions are also the conditions for "symbolic action," as distinct from sheer nonsymbolic motion (as with the kinds of cosmic and geological events that would go on, if there were no symbol-using animals).

No individual "things" exist in isolation. They are parts of wider "contexts," and no two such contexts are identical; also, by reason of their differences in time, place, and "history," no two things are in an identical relationship to any universal, infinite context. Accordingly things can but be *analogous* to one another.

There is a sense in which the human body is reducible to its context; in being composed, for instance, of the same chemical elements as are found outside the body, it is *continuous* with its context. But the body is *discontinuous* with its context (its "environment") in the sense that, in being characterized by the "centrality of the nervous system," each person's experiences, or sensations, are uniquely immediate to that person alone, however closely they may resemble (be analogous to) other persons' uniquely immediate experiences or sensations.

Empirically, the human person could be defined as a kind of animal organism, the centrality of whose nervous system provides a physiological principle of individuation (reducible to terms of sheer motion). It is endowed by mutation with a trait differing from all other known animals, namely, the ability and need to communicate with the aid of an arbitrary, conventional symbol-system (such as a tribal language) of such a nature that it can comment on itself; and this aptitude, or necessity, sets up the conditions for *symbolic action*, as distinct from mere motion. It is this "second-level" dimension (the possibility of words-about-words, symbols-about-symbols) that makes possible the development of human personality as we know it; the trait is not necessarily honorific; it can lead to modes of misconduct that compare wretchedly indeed with the decencies of nonhuman animal behavior. Also, the distinction is purely empirical, in the sense that further research might establish a similar trait in some other species, though at present we do not know of such.

All this is a ponderously expanded way of saying that the Dramatistic model is based upon the primary intuition that *persons act* (and that, accordingly, the model of human motivation should be designed as a heuristic device to make clear what is implicit in the idea of an act). Though such an expression as "All the world's a stage" would be a metaphor, a Dramatistic model would be applied quite differently. It would serve, rather, as an aid for helping us find answers to the question "What related observations follow from the proposition that 'man is a person, who can act, as distinct from things that can but move'?" It is good drama to say that "All the world's a stage." But Dramatism is not drama; it is the systematic use of a model designed to help us define and place the nature of human relationships and of the relations among our terms for the discussion of such matters.

To move from the observation that "a character in a play acts in character" to a corresponding concern with an "agent-act ratio" is by no means to be speaking metaphorically. There *literally is* some

Kenneth Burke

kind of consistency between a man's character and his actions. Similarly, there *literally is* a "scene-act ratio," involving respects in which men's acts are influenced, or are interpreted as being influenced, by their situations.

The study of the forms underlying rhetoric, poetic, and philosophy (including religion) makes it obvious that the realm of symbolic action introduces motivational complexities not reducible to a simple concern with "contingencies of reinforcement" such as B. F. Skinner's Behaviorism makes so much of (and there is no denying the force of such conditioning). Skinner so arranges a situation that experimental animals are able to learn a set of *motions* whereby they can keep from starving. Though much symbolic activity is involved in his arranging of such situations, there is no symbolic interchange at all between him and the animals. He asks them nothing, he tells them nothing, he does not argue with them as he does with his opponents. He simply sets up a "behave or starve" situation, and that's that.

The irony underlying his book *Beyond Freedom and Dignity* is that it could be interpreted as actually revealing reasons why his "engineering" technique would *not* work with humans. As I read his book, he is dealing with much the same motivational contradiction that I was concerned with in my essay "War, Response, and Contradiction" (republished in *Philosophy of Literary Form*), except that I view the contradiction as permanently intrinsic to human motivation. I have in mind the fact that one can advocate a cause either by detailing the advantages to be gained if it triumphs, or by depicting people who consent to be sacrificed in its behalf. I also discuss the same point in *Permanence and Change* (cf. "The Peace-War Conflict," pp. 197-98), when noting that man is motivated by contradictory ideals of both ease and strain (though I would now want to replace "peace" by some such word as "relaxation," and "war" by "stress").

Basically, I suspect, Skinner's behavioristic determinism is based on such over-simplified assumptions of "rationality" as are possible only to one of his pigeons, pecking like crazy to hit the jackpot that will be released if the bird manages to make the necessary discriminations at top speed and gobbles down the few bits of grain as fast as possible, to be ready for the next ordeal.

As I see it, a Dramatistic model of symbolic action is not a metaphor, at least not in the sense that Turbayne's view of things as words is. Or, at the very least, it avoids the overly *naturalistic* limitations of Turbayne's metaphor, even as corrected by "awareness." For his metaphor deflects our attention from the full range of observations (in poetics, rhetoric, philosophy, and human relations generally) that derive from a stress upon "the implications of the

30

idea of an act," a more *social* emphasis, as befits the essentially social nature of language, or "symbolicity" in general. Obviously, a view of things as words is metaphorical; but a definition of man as the symbol-using animal is literal, even so literal that it would allow us to go along quite sympathetically with the conceit of *things* as being in a sense the *"signs* of words" (cf. "What Are the Signs of What?" *Language as Symbolic Action*, pp. 359-79).

To make a choice between the proposition that "persons act" and "humans are machines that but move" is not the same as with James's "will to believe," or Pascal's "wager." It is empirically obvious that one does not relate to machines by persuasion, and no Don Juan ever got hot enough to try making a machine love him. If a mechanist literally believed that his associates were identical with factory products, he'd go crazy (or, to be more accurate, he'd already be crazy). It is those who reduce everything to terms of motion who are guilty of a metaphor. We relate to one another as persons (hence they must be persuaded in all sorts of symbol-using ways not reducible to "contingencies of reinforcement"). And thereupon the Dramatistic model is needed, to open up the whole realm of human motivation, since the Old Adam in man is essentially Dramatistic, even to the extent that he sometimes writes dramas available to use as models, not in the sense of information about this or that regarding mankind, but in the sense of revealing formal principles intrinsic to symbolicity as a motivational dimension.

Yet, hold! We must never forget that, however social the nature of symbolic action is, the life of the individual as defined by the centrality of his nervous system is grounded empirically in the realm of sheer motion. When his heart stops moving for good, he's through. I say this because I must always be on guard lest my great concern with the range of symbolic acts be misinterpreted to imply that my views end in idealism. In this regard I consider myself wholly an understudy of Santayana who, even while doing so handsomely by the realm of "spirit" (in my terms, "symbolic action") took it as beyond question that such "spirit" is *grounded* in "matter" ("sheer motion"). But though we die when the motions within us die, above that "materialistic" likelihood there have arisen the wonders and vexations made possible by man's symbolic prowess, as *literally* revealed by the Dramatistic model.

In conclusion I might add: the treatment of "topics" in Aristotle's *Rhetoric* strikes me as at the very center of the Dramatistic, though his *Poetics* mentions the *Rhetoric* only with reference to one qualitative part of tragedy, "thought" *(dianoia)*. I have in mind the fact that so many of the topics are like recipes for character, particularly insofar as, in a drama the recipes would not be merely spoken, but could be embedded in the very structure of the action. The most obvious examples are the recipes in Book II, for ways of inducing anger, mildness, friendship, hatred, fear, confidence, pity, indignation, etc. For the dramatist could be shown to build characters and dramatic situations by imitations associated with such "topics." Incidentally, we might recall that in the *Poetics* itself (section 15) the formulas for "character" are at a much higher level of generalization than with the *Rhetoric's* treatment of *ethos* and *pathos*.

Coda

Some basic propositions about Dramatism, as a philosophy of language:

1. Man's animality is in the realm of motion.
2. Man's symbolicity is in the realm of action.
3. Animality, the realm of motion, is the *ground* of a few rudimentary purposes, such as the desire for food, shelter, rest, sexual gratification, freedom of motion, rights to make choices of one's own.
4. When you add the complications of symbolic action, a near-infinity of *ad interim* purposes becomes available, an exceptionally rational and irrational one being the drive to accumulate atop accumulation atop accumulation the counters of mounting power.
5. Another such overall purpose, closely related, is the goad to acquire authority of one sort or another. Perhaps this is ultimately a reflex of communication as a motive, though in various ways and to a varying extent it can lead to the opposite results.
6. But intrinsic to all such variations of communication in terms of symbol-systems, there is conceivably a generating principle that is purely formal.
7. There would be such insofar as man confronts a basic division between the realms of the symbolic and the nonsymbolic.
8. In keeping with his specific nature as the symbol-using animal, he necessarily sees the nonsymbolic realm (of motion) *in terms of* the symbolic mediums through which he contemplates the nonsymbolic realm and thereby in effect *translates* it.
9. Thus what we call man's "anthropomorphism" is ultimately the logic (or better, the logologic) of reduction to symbolicity.
10. Such reduction in terms is ultimately reducible to the *principle of the sentence*. (Elsewhere I have made this point in verse: "We are sentenced to the sentence.")
11. That principle in turn is reducible to a matter of meaning—for if a sentence would live up to its ultimate possibilities, thereby

being perfectly, formally, a sentence, it must *mean* something.

12. But "meaning" is the ideal logological synonym for purpose. (We see this in the usage whereby we so readily shift between the words used in a question such as "What do you mean?" and a sentence such as "What do you mean to do?" (That is, "What do you *intend* to do?")

13. Apply the pattern thus to the world in general (give it its entelechical fulfillment) and you are goaded to ask such questions as, "What is the meaning of life? What is its purposes?"

14. Thereby you ask a question that would reduce the realms of both symbolic and nonsymbolic to the essence of symbolism, the *meaning* of an all-inclusive sentence.

The answer, or evasions and perversions of an answer, are (like the Devil) legion. Another way of proposing answers is to offer (most often metaphorically) a summarizing statement as to "what man is."

Here is an illustrative, random list:

Life is a pilgrimage. Life is a first draft, with constant revisions that are themselves first drafts. Life is the answer to a call not clearly understood, nor did the lostling know just where it came from. Life is a dream, or a carnival, or a labyrinth. Man is the political animal, man is to man a wolf, man is a featherless biped, or a vertical mammal. Life is an unending dialogue; when we enter, it's already going on; we try to get the drift of it; we leave before it's over. Man is but a mechanism. Life is a series of prerequisite courses, in which we are all drop-outs. Life for one man I knew was a speeding that came to a grinding halt. For another it was an insomniac somnambulism.

All possible such summings up can be but fragmentary, since we are but fragments, yet somehow related to a whole. But what of an attitude that offers us an overall *purpose*?

I can offer only one that seems to make wholly rational sense. And to a large extent it has been given to us by the fact that our great prowess with the resources of symbolic action led to the astounding ingenious inventions of technology.

Now, owing to technology's side-effect, pollution, mankind clearly has one unquestionable purpose; namely, to seek for ways and means (with correspondingly global attitudes) of undoing the damage being caused by man's failure to control the powers developed by his own genius.

His machines are not just the *fruits* of human rationality. They are in a sense the *caricature* of his rationality.

With the great flowering of technology, the problem of self-control takes on a possibly fatal new dimension. Man must so control his invented servants that they cease to control him.

Until man solves that problem, he has purpose a-plenty.

The Arts of Indirection

Maurice Natanson

It was important to him that there should be some "friendly faces" in his classes. He often remarked that he liked a certain "face" and he wanted that face to be there even if the person said nothing.
Ludwig Wittgenstein: A Memoir
by Norman Malcolm

The conviction which underlies this paper is that there is an internal connection between what we learn and the way in which we learn it, and that the way of learning points back to the peculiar stance of the teacher. It may be that some subjects are less affected by such a connection than others. Certainly, I have no wish to argue that the study of sanitary engineering is vitally related to the nature of the professor of that discipline. But I believe it to be self-evident that, for anyone who has studied the lives of Max Weber and Karl Jaspers, it is virtually impossible to comprehend the core of Jaspers's thought without attending in a serious way to his complex relationship with Weber. It is not a matter of selecting names. Rather I suggest that the problems of the bond between teacher and student extend far beyond the surface and obvious phenomena of stimulation, encouragement, and criticism. There may well be a proper psychology of study; there is also, however, a philosophy of learning. It is my hope that something of that philosophy will become clear in the ensuing analysis. It might be useful to point out now that my interest in the realm of "indirection" is wide-ranging and somewhat scattered. I intend to resist the temptation to focus my remarks on one thinker, such as Kierkegaard, who might otherwise serve the function of providing a historical and textual matrix in which an examination of indirection might prosper. Part of the reason I choose to look into divergent fields comes from the interdisciplinary character of this occasion. Another and perhaps more important reason for the concept-hopping which will follow is that I believe that indirection is best approached in a somewhat tortuous fashion. The risk I take is that you may conclude that I have tried to do too much far too swiftly. To that charge I plead guilty in advance. However, the advantage I foresee in pursuing the strategy I have decided on is that an inroad into a remote region of thought, an

This essay is dedicated to Ernst Manasse

almost forgotten path toward self-comprehension, may be opened up or recovered.

I wish to understand indirection in the broadest sense. Most simply, it is the pursuit of an intersubjective truth in a distinctively subjective way. *The* truth is approached by way of *my* truth; but the striking implication of that notion is that *your* truth may find its liberation for you in virtue of *our* efforts. The impulse of indirection, then, is social; the concern is not idiosyncratic but public. Yet the fulfillment of what indirection promises lies beyond the province of the individual. I intend to explore indirection in a variety of settings. In each case the task will be to locate something of its dynamic and structure. It should be clear that the sphere in which I will treat my theme is essentially methodological. By that I mean nothing more, for the moment, than the interest in the nature and ramifications of indirection rather than its detailed applications. It might be prudent to say that methodology, as I interpret it, is far from being an esoteric or even highly specialized enterprise. To the contrary, we will soon observe indirection at work in its native soil, harvesting strength from disparate yet familiar sources. I propose to examine four spheres in which indirection operates: mundanity, rhetoric, philosophy, and pedagogy. In a sense, there is an art proper to each of these spheres, and so I shall be investigating indirection as a mundane art, as a rhetorical art, as a philosophical art, and as a pedagogic art. These are the arts of indirection. I shall turn to them as representatives but not exhaustive illustrations of their kind. Please wish me well as I proceed!

Indirection as a Mundane Art

By "mundanity" I understand the character of the everyday world, the flow of naive experience which we all tacitly recognize as daily life. Edmund Husserl refers to mundanity in terms of the "life-world." Within the texture of our ordinary believing in the reality and efficacy of everydayness, we construct the familiar reality of day to day existence. As I have suggested, such construction is not a reflective or self-conscious procedure. It is rather the case that man in the current of daily life simply "takes for granted"—to use Alfred Schutz's telling phrase—the order and implications of his typifications of social reality. There is, of course, a genesis to such typification. From childhood on, the individual develops "recipes" for meeting the demands of social existence, for meeting the requirements of social roles, and even for anticipating the unexpected. Such "recipes"—another term borrowed from Schutz—are abstractions from any concretely, historically given phenomenon. It is legitimate to trace out the career of "recipe-accumulation" in the history of the individual in the taken-for-granted world, but it is equally important to recognize that recipes are composed of elements which are drawn from what I would call the physiognomy of daily life. Before we learn what "good" behavior is for a child, we know something about admonitions in general and warning looks in particular. I can remember being taken by my mother when I was about five or six years old to make a formal call on some distant relative. We were seated in a most sedate living room, furnished with what I now realize must have been antiques. The lady we were visiting sat on one antique chair, my mother sat on a second antique chair, and I sat on a third antique chair. Following the usual perfunctory inquiry about how I liked school, the adults set about the business of conversing between themselves. After a while, I moved about in my chair, which then gave a small but distinctive creak. The woman looked at me. A few minutes later, I moved again. Another creak. This time the looks changed from civil tolerance to the onset of a glare. A third creak brought the news of potential catastrophe to the face of our relative: the unspoken accusation that I was a Chippendale crippler. My mother suggested that I go outside to play.

The "looks" one gets in situations of that sort are understood before the "recipe" of how to act when visiting is mastered fully by a child. Admonitions have their own history. The physiognomy of daily life is built up from signals and signs sequestered in or revealed by the stance of persons, the legends of home and street, and the accents of motion and work. Social roles may be understood, in these terms, as higher-level complexes of significant gesture. Jurgen Ruesch and Weldon Kees write in their interesting book on *Nonverbal Communication:*

> The recognition of *roles* is implemented through the perception and interpretation of a variety of strategic cues. The speediest assignment of a role becomes possible when custom or circumstances determines the use of uniforms and one person is able to address another as "Officer," "Waiter," "Nurse," or "Sergeant." Roles may be indicated also through material objects; tools, implements, and machines sometimes identify such persons as welders, musicians, or brakemen. Sometimes a variety of cues throws light on the identification of members of particular trades—when uniforms, props, movements, and even language characteristics contribute to identification. Usually, however, such identification is far more complex, since any one person may fulfill multiple roles at the same time—roles defined in terms of age, sex, occupation, family position, citizenship—and may shift through a number of such transient roles as those of a pedestrian, passenger, spectator, or consumer. The cues singled out and fixed upon are also determined not only by the subjective needs and expectations of the participants but by the total context of the situation.[1]

Roles, on this account, prove to be both results of indirect communication and conditions for indirect communication. We see a patch of uniform, a badge, a distinctive cap, and quickly we are poised for an encounter—however trivial—with authority or with delegates of the menial. At the same time, the signs of office are interpreted as schemas through which we organize our attitudes to large segments of the social world. It is tacitly assumed on the part of all of us who are part of daily life that order and coherence are embedded in sociality, that the emblems of the social signify prein-terpreted codes of action whose meaning constitutes the familiarity of the taken-for-granted world of everyday existence. Ruesch and Kees identify a variety of social situations in which interpretive cues are presented at quite rudimentary levels of interrelationship. For example, in a "service situation" where a bootblack is shining the customer's shoes, cues are "derived from background, equipment, costume, and posture."[2] In a "conversational situation," cues are "derived from grouping and gestures."[3] In a "play situation," there is derivation from "prop, age, and activity,"[4] whereas in a "family situation," cues are "derived from age, sex, grouping, and the ways in which the participants face each other."[5] The bootblack's sign may directly announce his activity, but the sign is the least impor-tant feature of his situation in the interpretive context. The essential character of the transaction taking place is indirectly given by way of stance, movement, and the large realm of gesture. Most often, there is no direct sign which announces human activities. Two people carrying on an ordinary conversation in the street do not have a sign about them which announces: "Conversation taking place." Some families may have a "God bless our home" sign hanging on the living room wall, but it would be odd to see a sign which said: "This is a home." Most men at work are not identified by a "Men at work" sign. Indeed, there is no label ever presented which tells us: "Daily life is going on here." The most critical features of sociation are presupposed, taken for granted, simply assumed by all of us most of the time. That vast assumption is at the root of mundane indirection.

It was George H. Mead who coined the insightful phrase "conver-sation of gestures." In a way, I am suggesting that such a conversa-tion goes on not only between animals or between human beings, but also between the situations of everydayness and the human reality which tacitly comprehends and responds to those situations. Strolling past two men conversing indirectly involves a recognition of their activity, a making room, as it were, for a fragment of daily life to live itself within the welter of mundane concerns. The modes of recognition include noting, witnessing, and even ignoring. Eaves-dropping is merely one way of appreciating the segment of experi-ence which responds to the onlooker or "onhearer" as a fugitive communicant in the world's conversation. But the conversation in question undergirds language. Gesture is the voice of mundanity, the speech of situations, the tongue of indirection. To converse, in these terms, is to enlarge the very sense of discourse by adding to our potential partners in communication the conduct of scenes and the landscape of social action taken at its most primal, gestural level.

Indirection as a Rhetorical Art

I am not especially interested, for present purposes, in trying to establish a definition of *rhetoric* or even in giving an account of how I am using the term for the discussion which follows. Elsewhere I have tried to examine the notion of rhetoric within a philosophic framework. It does not seem to me to be useful to start still another foray in that battle. Perhaps it will suffice to say that by rhetoric I have in mind the locus of language as a human instrumentality in effecting action between men, whether they be speakers and listeners or writers and readers. In what follows, I shall turn to the writer-reader relationship as the paradigm for my analysis. And it may safely be said at the outset that the paradigm I have chosen is indeed a problematic one. The reasons for its being problematic are these: first, the activity which we call "writing" is mysterious; second, the status of the product of writing—the novel, let us say— is ambiguous; and third, the identity and function of the reader as well as the nature of the activity of reading are obscure. What is it to write? and For whom does one write? are, as Jean-Paul Sartre has shown, intrinsically disturbing questions. Sartre begins his book *What is Literature?* by distinguishing between the poet and the proseman. "I would readily define the prose-writer," Sartre says, "as a man who *makes use* of words."[6] "Poets," on the contrary, "are men who refuse to *utilize* language."[7] He goes on to say:

> For the poet, language is a structure of the external world. The speaker
> is *in a situation* in language; he is invested with words. They are
> prolongations of his meanings, his pincers, his antennae, his
> eyeglasses. He maneuvers them from within; he feels them as if they
> were his body; he is surrounded by a verbal body which he is hardly
> aware of and which extends his action upon the world. The poet is
> outside of language. He sees words inside out as if he did not share the
> human condition, and as if he were first meeting the word as a barrier as
> he comes toward men. Instead of first knowing things by their name, it
> seems that first he has a silent contact with them, since, turning toward
> that other species of thing which for him is the word, touching them,
> testing them, palping them, he discovers in them a slight luminosity of
> their own and particular affinities with the earth, the sky, the water, and
> all created things.[8]

The utilization of language, then, presupposes language itself. No matter how remarkable and devastating the prose writer is, his performance remains within language; language is ultimately at his disposal. The poet, on the other hand, must reconstruct language in order to enter the world. For him, the word is haunted by its possibilities. Further, the word is discovered and recovered by a groping toward its eternal and continuous genesis. The poet is a "gropeman" of infant and collapsed stars of language. As Günter Eich has written: "In each good line of poetry I hear the cane of the blindman striking.⁹

Whether or not Sartre's distinction between prose and poetry holds up, I would suggest that the radical indirection he ascribes to the poet in search of language filters through at least in derivative ways in writing, whether poetry or prose, which turns toward itself in an effort to reseize the world. In Joyce, in Beckett, in Barthelme, language is accused, tried, *sentenced*. Only a general amnesty would bring from their cells the words we have punished. We are living in a time in which the deterioration of language in the mundane sphere is a challenge to the writer who accepts the task of reconstructing the world through the artifice of the very language which has failed us. The search for new connections between writer and reader hinges on the capacity of the one to relocate the other in his presence to the world. Nowhere, in my judgment, is this better exemplified than in the work of James Agee. His rhetorical art is a celebration of indirection.

Agee's (and Walker Evans's) *Let Us Now Praise Famous Men* was published six years before Sartre's *What Is Literature*? In a different way, Agee is concerned with essentially the same problems which trouble Sartre. Remembering Sartre's distinction between the writer of prose and the writer of poetry, consider the following passage from *Let Us Now Praise Famous Men*:

> Words cannot embody; they can only describe. But a certain kind of artist, whom we will distinguish from others as a poet rather than a prose writer, despises this fact about words or his medium, and continually brings words as near as he can to an illusion of embodiment. In doing so he accepts a falsehood but makes, of a sort in any case, better art. It seems very possibly true that art's superiority over science and over all other forms of human activity, and its inferiority to them, reside in the identical fact that art accepts the most dangerous and impossible of bargains and makes the best of it, becoming, as a result, both nearer the truth and farther from it than those things which, like science and scientific art, merely describe, and those things which, like human beings and their creations and the entire state of nature, merely are, the truth.¹⁰

Agee's "illusion of embodiment" is a metaphor for indirection as a rhetorical art. The writer strives to approach in language what human beings *are* in fact: centers of being which bear an ultimately incorruptible truth—that each of us exists, that each existent is itself and not any other, that identity, like divinity, is a sovereign and transcendent force. Ragpickers of language may balk at Agee's insistencies. That each of us exists may seem and indeed be judged to be the most banal of claims; that each existent is itself and not any other may be thought to be, at best, a repetition of Bishop Butler's dictum; that identity is a sovereign and transcendent force may appear to rehearse what is least comprehensible about the divinity Agee likens us to. In the end, we may be told that the trouble with Agee's writing is his rhetoric. Some response to such criticism is necessary.

I believe that writing embodies a tension between the utilization and the recreation of language. At first blush, the proseman has words at his service; selecting them seems to be the chief problem. On closer examination, it is the distance between the writer and language, between the writing and the reader, which throws into relief the artist's uncertain stance with regard to his craft. The source of indirection in both writer and reader is the always potential rift between what we have as language and what we may attain through language. Agee builds his case for language on the ground of language which refines itself to steel in the furnace of what otherwise might seem to be romanticism. The rhetorical force of his art consists in the overextension, the overweighting of words which attempt to carry the reader to the far side of his own experience. The point to which we are driven by Agee is the recognition of others—fellow human creatures whose lost and damaged realities are continuous with and, finally, identical with our own fractured being. Rhetoric here is the laceration of language in the name of human solidarity.

Indirection as a Philosophical Art

As a philosophical theme, indirection constitutes an interior moment in the development of thought, for it is part of philosophy's necessary concern with its own procedures which establishes the self-reflective character of philosophical work. The philosopher turns to the problems of communication not out of special interest but out of necessity. It is obvious from the history of philosophy that the methods employed in the pursuit of truth are not only qualitatively varied—everything from poems and dialogues to question and answer lists and treatises—but are recognized as posing difficulties for the inquirer. It is one thing to locate the most authoritative, recent text on thoracic surgery; it is another matter altogether to ask for the most authoritative, recent text on metaphysics. Good books can usually be recommended, but a host of qualifications needs to be introduced to give the potential reader some idea of what sort of approach he is going to find in a treatise on metaphysics written by a Thomist or a neo-Hegelian. Above all, some appeal to experience is called for in philosophical work. The student of surgery may be able to pick up where his predecessors have left off; the student of philosophy must start all over again, must, in Edmund Husserl's terms, become a *beginner*. Clearly, the closer one comes to existential issues the less likely it is that the reports others have made can be relied on. The individual must find his own way. That quick sentence brings us to Kierkegaard.

In the writings of the Danish philosopher, the relationship between direct and indirect discourse is an overpowering theme. As Walter Lowrie points out, "S. K. maintained that 'direct communication,' which seeks to impart truth by simply communicating 'results,' is not possible with regard to such truths as most deeply concern a man (viz., ethical and religious truths); for in this case not only *what* one learns but *how* one appropriates it is of importance. Such truths must be appropriated subjectively and by one's own effort." [11] What this means for Kierkegaard as a writer is that his philosophic task consists of guiding his reader in such a way that the reader is not *led* but liberated. Indirection is the means for bringing the individual to the moment of self-comprehension. Thus, Kierkegaard's strategy is to undercut the traditional means by which an author instructs his reader. A host of devices serves that strategy: pseudonymous names in authorship, variant voices in the chant of irony, titles which revolt against expectation, images and anecdotes which confound the serious and trip the pompous. An author may examine the ways in which salvation may be secured, but Kierkegaard has given up security in favor of that splendid isolation in which the distance between *my* and *your* is honored. If there is a conclusion in S. K.'s work, it is that the individual must confront and engage his own inwardness. Such a conclusion makes it impossible for the reader to say: "I do exactly as Kierkegaard did." Or as Kierkegaard himself expressed it: "I want no disciples."

Although Kierkegaard may be called the philosopher of indirection, it should not be assumed that he is the only figure in the history of philosophy who merits the title, nor is it the case that indirection is always to be found on so exalted a level. Communication between philosophers and between philosophers and their audiences includes some tacky and marginal procedures. The manipulation of a situation may come through the use of derision, jokes, laughter, and references to earlier efforts by a philosopher which may have met with failure of one kind or another. There may be resorts to even less legitimate techniques: interruption, dramatic shifts in bodily posture, making faces, or, should worst come to worst, trumpet-like nose-blowing. Of course, it may be said that such devices are not instruments of indirection but refusals to permit genuine philosophical discourse to occur. There is certainly some truth to that. My point is that for philosophers who may not display much sympathy with Kierkegaardian indirection, there are still efforts to divert an audience—efforts which appear to be outside the scope of philosophy but which are relied on not infrequently for whatever indirect help they provide. The philosopher who would be quick to discount verbal trickery nevertheless participates in a discussion which has an extraphilosophical life of its own in which persuasion and beguilement by all sorts of chicanery matter. Indirection creeps in through the trap door of discourse.

The appeal to authority, in some instances, is a tacit move toward indirection. We are taught in logic, of course, that an argument which says in effect, "Accept this because I am in charge here" is not convincing. Of course, what logic rejects, common sense has long accepted in certain aspects of daily life. What child has never heard from its parent in response to a request for the rationale of a demand or a position: "Because I'm your mother!" "Because I'm your father!"? It is very difficult to explain what that means, but it is more often than not, I suspect, the case that "Because I'm your mother!" is spoken with an emphasis which tends to validate the assertion. It is as if the speaker were saying, "There is a connection between us which justifies my demand and which cannot itself be challenged." In other words, the fallacy of the appeal to authority arises only when the authority is someone other than your mother. Something of the same élitist logic may be encountered outside the home. In his book on Bertrand Russell, Rupert Crawshay-Williams writes:

> Certainly, when I started learning philosophy from Russell and others I noticed that there was a curious mixture of tentativeness and confidence in the way in which philosophical views were stated: philosophical *theories* would be put forward in a tone which allowed that alternative views, though wrong, might nevertheless have points in their favour and would be listened to in a gentlemanly manner. The initial *premises* though (that is, the assumptions about proper usage and rules of reasoning which underlay the whole discussion) were in a very different case: they would be put forward (if at all—many of them would of course remain unstated) in a tone of emphasis which took them completely for granted—so much so that any attempt to question them would be met at first with unconcealed astonishment and then quite often with the assertion or re-assertion in a loud and confident voice of the proposition in question. [12]

"Because I'm your Russell!" would seem to be the message of astonishment and a raised voice. In the case of Russell (as in the case of your father), the message is quite effective: the inquirer is silenced or squashed. But it is evident that squashing is not synonymous with answering or defending. What has happened is that an argument has led us away from its terms to the person who proclaims those terms. The logic books call this a fallacy. I am concerned with pointing out something about such a procedure which has less to do with logical validity than with the deployment of indirection in philosophical discourse. Challenging Russell's assumptions means challenging Russell. It has been pointed out, of course, that challenging G. E. Moore's assumptions did not entail challenging G. E. Moore. Yet a quiet and humanely detached "What on earth can you possibly mean by that?" may be still a different turn on the path of indirection. I have been trying to follow out bits of that trail in these small excursions.

Indirection as a Pedagogic Art

The discussion of authority has already brought us to the realm of pedagogy. The teacher is present to the student both as a representative of his discipline and as an individual who will lead or guide the student in his development. The relationship may be profound. Earlier, I mentioned Jaspers's relationship to Weber. That may serve as a clue to profundity as an existential relationship. In an impressive essay, Ernst Moritz Manasse has developed the idea of Jaspers's connection with Weber as being analogous to Plato's connection with Socrates. Manasse writes:

> As Plato saw it, Socrates emphasized the limits of nondialectical thinking in order to make room for the *docta ignorantia* which is the beginning of true philosophy. As Jaspers sees it, Max Weber pointed out the limits of empirical science in order to protect the *"existential"* freedom of the individual from the encroachments of the cogent. Weber's negations, as do Socrates', have a positive aim. Instead of stopping the flight of the spirit they are to stimulate it. Weber's determined separation of the scientifically knowable from what belongs to the realm of personal evaluation aims at more than the contrast between the rational and the irrational which leaves the latter without light and responsibility. On the contrary, Weber's whole energies were directed at narrowing the sphere of the irrational. In a gigantic effort he attempted to gather all the light which reason provides and to focus it on the secret sources of our choices and decisions. Thus he pointed to the true freedom while engaging his whole strength in the service of the un-ending rational analysis. Weber's example, like Socrates', inspired those who were susceptible to the greatness of such an undertaking. In no one did it produce a more profound effect than in Jaspers. Just as Plato's philosophy could be interpreted as his attempt to say what he had experienced through Socrates, so it is possible to consider Jaspers' thinking as his way of expressing what he had experienced through Max Weber. [13]

It is important not to interpret Jaspers's relationship to Weber in terms of discipleship. To the contrary, it was precisely because he was not a disciple and because no one could be Weber's disciple that Jaspers was able to establish his existential bond with a master. In his response to Manasse's essay, Jaspers makes this point directly. He writes:

> On one occasion [Friedrich] Gundolf said to me: "Had I not been a disciple of [Stefan] George, I would have become one of Weber." To which I replied: "That's just it, to become a Weberian is impossible." Everyone who would be so stupid as to want to become his disciple, did not comprehend him. Max Weber met everyone on principle *al pari*; he referred any young man, who had the impulse of wanting to become a disciple, back to himself and to his own freedom. Discipleship is disastrous and cannot be carried through in truthfulness. [14]

The authority of the master consists in his being able to sustain an existential relationship with the student without permitting discipleship. The only way one could "follow" Weber would be to rethink one's way to him and through him by pursuing one's own intellectual and human career. Although the language of indirection does not appear in the Manasse-Jaspers discussion, I think that it is deeply present. The model Jaspers presents us with is that of authority which does not say, "Follow me because I'm your father!" but rather states, in effect, "Turning to me for instruction must mean freeing yourself *by* the bond you bear to me." The bond is freedom; the bond is existential relationship. The student works his way toward himself through the life of his teacher.

No doubt, authority may, on occasion, proceed in quite different ways. There are practical needs to be met by any teacher who tries to instruct a student. At times what is called for is the narrower command: "If you respect me, accept what I say!" Once again, it is easy to confuse this kind of demand with the most illicit form of the appeal to authority. The legitimate use of "respect me" comes into play in certain situations where the student must "accept" a doctrine in order to be able to challenge it. The best illustration I can offer for such "acceptance" is a story I was told some years ago by a student of Husserl. The student had asked Husserl about the phenomenological concept of "appresentation," the idea that in seeing an object, we see it as *backed*—not that we see the unseen side but that the unseen side is *appresented*. The notion is a difficult one and is open to easy misunderstanding as well as to cheap ridicule. Husserl's student asked him how it was possible to see the backed aspect of the object. Now it would have been perfectly proper for the philosopher to reply at length, going through the kind of explanation he gives in *Cartesian Meditations*. Instead, his face grew threatening, his eyes scorching, his beard menacing. "I see it!" he roared. The bookshelves in his study trembled, the history of philosophy seemed about to come down on the student like an avalanche, all of

Freiburg shook. In fearful response the student blurted: "Oh yes, Herr Geheimrat, I see it too!" Husserl knew the student would have a philosophical lifetime to think over the matter and decide for himself. What he gave him for the moment was the conviction that here was something which mattered.

The art of philosophical indirection consists, then, in a commitment by the teacher to the student's freedom, especially in those instances where the student wants the teacher to tell him what to do. In refusing to dominate his student, the teacher is at the same time refusing to be a guru. Indirection, interpreted as a phenomenological theme, amounts to a conviction put into action that *beginning* in philosophy is the proper and really inevitable task the student must face for himself. Moreover, beginning means turning to one's own concrete reality, to the phenomena of immediate experience as lived and encountered in the course of the individual's career. It should be obvious that indirection is neither a substitute for the study of the history of philosophy nor a surrogate for analytic inquiry. Rather, indirection is the point of *being* a teacher and of standing in relationship to a fellow human being who is trying to find his own entrance to the realm of philosophical endeavor. That such an interpretation carries with it a strong existential motif has already been suggested. Jaspers's relationship to Weber was existential. That may mean ultimately that in order to understand a teacher it is necessary to love him. As Manasse writes: "Jaspers' philosophy is rooted in his communication with Max Weber. This means that one cannot speak of an influence of Max Weber on Jaspers as of an element which could be separated from the rest of Jaspers' thinking. Communication means an *'existential'* relation, means loving communion in search of truth."[15] The conclusion which follows is that "in order to know Weber one has to love him."[16] Indirection has taken us from Weber's texts to the human reality at the source of those texts. Love proves to be a hidden feature of philosophy. Every once in a while, the philosopher catches up with the meaning of the word which stands for what he does.

It is time to conclude. The arts I have been describing are concerned with indirection in the varying contexts of daily life, language, philosophy, and teaching. Not only do the contexts vary, but the meaning of indirection changes with each art. I have no wish to transform unyielding material into a uniform pattern. Still, there is some continuity in the nature of indirection in the four arts we have investigated. In all cases, indirection points to an unsuspected second path which shadows our usual walk. Mundane reality becomes a partner in an unimagined conversation; language displays a rhetorical dimension which connives in the reconstruction of poetry and, ultimately, prose; philosophy sets us in the direction of beginning and demands that we pass through our teachers; and those teachers, finally, follow a demon of their own who insists that authority be exercised in the cause of freedom. In all of these instances, it is the case that indirection involves the primacy of the *how* over the *what* of experience. There should be no misunderstanding at this point. I am saying that in daily life, language, philosophy, and teaching, the way in which we act, write, think, and learn is bound to the content of experience. Individuation is something to be achieved; it cannot be legislated. Accordingly, indirection is an art rather than a technique. Even where it is used self-consciously and for specific purposes, as with Kierkegaard, the philosopher subordinates his method to his purpose: the arousal of the alter ego.

It does not follow that because indirection is an art of the spheres we have examined, it is the only art. Nor have I maintained that direct discourse is somehow inferior or lacking in quality or efficacy. To the contrary, I believe that indirection functions in a world which rightly demands other modes of communication. Asking the grocer for a quart of milk, following the instructions for completing tax returns, learning what Hume had to say about causation, and going to school are as much moments of or pieces of the experiential world as are the arts of indirection. But it would be unwise to ignore the other side of discourse in which primal and existential relationships are in question. Even if we remain rooted in common sense, we need not avoid the oblique truth which mundanity reveals: the way in which we come to experience shapes what we experience. In some respects, daily life is the repository of our compromises with indirection. A final story may show what I mean.

I once had a graduate student many years ago whose field was psychology but who got interested in Sartre's ontology. Some of his fellow psychology students noticed the big book he was carrying around. "What's that?" they asked. "Why," he replied, "that's *Being and Nothingness*." Not long afterwards he was called in for a chat with the chairman of the psychology department. "Why are you reading *Being and Nothingness*?" the chairman asked. "Oh, it's very interesting," replied the student. An avuncular little discussion ensued in which the chairman counselled the student to give up reading Sartre. 'You have a good future in psychology," the chairman said, "don't endanger it." Now do you suppose that my student faced an existential choice, that he went through a dark night of the soul, that he fought off belligerent psychologists like a Kierkegaardian Douglas Fairbanks? Not a bit of it! He simply borrowed the dust jacket from a fat book on the psychology of learning, transferred it to *Being and Nothingness*, and was never bothered again.

From Philosophy to Rhetoric and Back

Henry W. Johnstone, Jr.

In this paper I want to discuss the development of my own ideas. It is not easy to see how to deal with this topic without giving the impression either that I am bragging or that I am confessing. But I am not an important enough person to engage in either activity in public. So I will attempt to achieve a certain impersonality by speaking of the arguments as such, minimizing their relationship with a living and self-referring propounder. Plato once wrote, "If the argument had a human voice, that voice would be heard laughing at us."[1] The occasion for this remark was a dialogue in the course of which the argument had forced Socrates and Protagoras to change sides. I want to think of arguments as autonomous agencies that a philosopher encounters—agencies indeed more often capable of laughing at him than bolstering his ego.

Let me try to explain my title. I will begin by outlining an initial view of the nature of philosophy. Then I will indicate an argument leading from this view to a certain conclusion concerning the nature of rhetoric. After that I want to consider arguments occasioning a revision in this theory of rhetoric. Finally, I will try to suggest an argument leading from this changed theory of rhetoric to a revised view of the nature of philosophy. Through argumentative routes we will have been led from philosophy to rhetoric and back. If arguments are agencies, they are travel agencies.

The starting point of this journey is the position that a philosophy, or at least a metaphysics, is an attempt to define what it is to be a fact. Thus if anyone wishes to attack a certain metaphysics, there are no facts to which he can appeal. Consider, for example, the vitalism of Bergson and how one might be tempted to attack it. Bergson held that whatever exists manifests the vital force, or, in short, life. To most people this would probably seem an outrageous claim. The universe, it might seem obvious, is strewn with bits of lifeless matter. The following fantasy is easy to indulge in: one picks up a rock, carries it into Bergson's study, thrusts it into his face, and says, with as much contempt as one can muster, "What do you think of this, professor?" (It was in the same spirit that Dr. Johnson kicked the stone in the attempt to refute the idealism of Berkeley.) But the alleged fact that a rock is lifeless is simply not a fact at all from Bergson's point of view. Nothing is lifeless. The rock in its own way manifests the vital force; it lives a degraded form of life. So the intruder into Bergson's study has begged the question. And similarly anyone who forces his way into any metaphysician's study carrying an alleged counter-example—a piece of matter, for example, or a Platonic Form—begs the question.

If philosophers define, in the manner indicated, what it is to be a fact, it is hard to see how discussions among the advocates of rival positions can occur at all. Each thinker basks in a universe he has defined himself, in splendid isolation from the definers of universes alien to his. Indeed, how can he even know that such counterdefinitions exist? His own principles prevent him from understanding them. One for whom all is life will be unable to distinguish the lifeless from life and hence to make sense of a view of reality in which the lifeless has a part to play.

But discussions do occur. Bergson argued with his critics. From that which I have said so far it follows that the arguments were not *ad rem*—they were not attempts to appeal to evidence. But there is another possibility. *Ad rem* arguments are often contrasted with those addressed *ad hominem*. (To put it differently, external criticism is contrasted with internal.) Instead of appealing to facts of dubious efficacy in overthrowing one's opponent's position, one might appeal directly to one's opponent's principles themselves. Instead of addressing ourselves to his position, we address ourselves to the intentions underlying his position. It is, of course, notoriously easy and tempting to argue invalidly in thus shifting the focus of the criticism. To attribute Bergson's position to his childhood experiences or to his ambition to publish is simply beside the point; the question is begged in this maneuver as egregiously as it is in showing Bergson the rock.

It is not my purpose here to propose any definitive criticism of Bergson. I only want to point out that certain lines of attack can be taken which are not obviously invalid. One might, for example, consider Bergson's claim that life can be understood intuitively but not in terms of discursive language. But does not Bergson's own prose—discursive writing at its best—belie this claim? We seem to have found an inconsistency between Bergson's position and his intention to express it.

What I am trying to develop at this point is an argument about arguments—a meta-argument. According to this meta-argument, if we assume that a philosophical position defines what it is to be a fact, and therefore cannot attack another position *ad rem*, then the only way in which it can engage in such an attack is *ad hominem*. Since *argumentum ad rem* and *argumentum ad hominem* do not exhaust the alternatives, this conditional is not a tautology. In addition to the *ad rem* and *ad hominem* appeals, there are appeals to force, authority, pity, sympathy, and so on. The meta-argument I am eliciting, however, assumes that these appeals are fallacious, at least in philosophical contexts, and accordingly cannot properly be used by one position to attack another. Only a nonfallacious appeal can be so used. Thus it must also be assumed that *argumentum ad hominem* is sometimes nonfallacious. It is so, according to the meta-argument, when it points to an actual inconsistency between the intentions of a thinker espousing the position under attack and that position itself.

The validity of this meta-argument is unfortunately by no means beyond question. For it is not at all clear what status is to be ascribed to the inconsistency exposed by an *argumentum ad hominem*. In speaking of it as "an actual inconsistency," as I did a moment ago, I have already suggested the difficulty. If the inconsistency is a fact, then to expose it is not to engage in an *argumentum ad hominem* after all; it is rather to use an *ad rem* argument. If the argument is a successful attack on the position it exposes as inconsistent with the intentions of the formulator of the position, then the nature of philosophy cannot be such as the meta-argument assumes. For there will then be a fact commonly acknowledged by several positions, each of which had been assumed to claim the exclusive right to define the facts; the fact, to wit, that one of the positions is inconsistent with the intentions of its propounder. Of course, the attack may well not succeed; if a philosophy does really claim to define what it is to be a fact, it will surely not be intimidated by somebody's contention that such-and-such is inconsistent. A thinker capable of seeing the nature of facts in his own way is surely not incapable of seeing the nature of inconsistencies in his own way. What is inconsistent for another may well not be inconsistent for him. So if the argument is after all *ad hominem*, there is every reason to suppose that it fails to accomplish its purpose. Of course, it may be possible to point out some meta-inconsistency between a thinker's intentions and his conception of inconsistency. But this poses the dilemma all over again at a new level. Either the argument exposing the meta-inconsistency is not *ad hominem* at all or it is invalid.

There are various ways of attempting to deal with this problem, but none of them, in the last analysis, succeeds. One way is to argue that in order for one position to attack another successfully, it is sufficient that they share a certain conception of inconsistency. But a conception of inconsistency shared by two conflicting positions need not be universal; it need not be shared by all positions. Hence the exposure of the inconsistency need not count as an appeal to fact.[2]

This argument, however, is in fact an *ignoratio elenchi*. The problem of accounting for the status of the inconsistency exposed by an *argumentum ad hominem* is not peculiarly occasioned by the need to appeal to a *universal* conception of inconsistency. It arises when *any* shared conception is appealed to. For an argument is *ad rem*, rather than *ad hominem*, as long as attacker and attackee both assume that the considerations appealed to by the attacker are facts; they need not *universally* be assumed to be facts. For example, if Socrates attacks Simmias's disbelief in the immortality of the soul by appealing to a notion of opposition shared by Simmias and him but not by us, Socrates is arguing *ad rem*. The situation here is that of two interlocutors neither of whom is attempting to define what it is to be a fact but both of whom operate within a universe of acknowledged fact.

There is another difficulty in this proposed solution. Suppose Position P_1 and Position P_2 have Conception C_1 of inconsistency in common. This may enable *them* to argue with each other, but unless C_1 is universal, it does not necessarily enable P_1 and P_3 or P_2 and P_3 to argue with each other. Assume that C_1 is not universal. Then some special conception of inconsistency, presumably not shared by P_1 and P_2, will have to be involved here. So P_1 will have to incorporate two distinct conceptions of inconsistency, one operating in its controversy with P_2 and the other underlying its argument with P_3. I do not think I need to go further. The situation simply gets too complicated to be plausible.

A more heroic recourse is to claim that one who attacks a position *ad hominem* can show that it is inconsistent in precisely the sense in which its propounder understands inconsistency, since the attacker stands within this conception of inconsistency as well as outside it.[3] He takes two positions concerning the nature of inconsistency—his own and that of his interlocutor—and these two positions are themselves inconsistent; they are not merely mutually supplementary. This approach to the problem obviously requires an unusual attitude toward some inconsistencies at least. The inconsistency between two views of inconsistency is apparently not regarded as a logical disaster, a defect to be corrected if the conversation is to continue at all. Yet that is of course the standard attitude toward a contradiction.

The unusual attitude arises in connection with a theory of selfhood. The self is said to come into being in the act in which a person occupies two inconsistent positions. The self is the perspective from which the poles of the contradiction are unified. Without this perspective, no contradiction could even be acknowledged as a contradiction. Without the contradiction, on the other hand, the self would never emerge.

The account I have given of this view is probably too sketchy to be of much use. But I think I have said enough about it to make clear one of its most urgent problems. The critic of a philosophical position who attacks it *ad hominem* does so by revealing an inconsistency between the position itself and the intentions of its advocate. In the light of this revelation, the advocate of the position is expected to abandon or revise it. In other words, his attitude toward his own inconsistency is supposed to be the standard attitude: the inconsistency must be removed before the discussion can go on. Yet at the same time, we are not expecting his attacker to take the standard attitude, for we see his own acknowledgment of his inconsistency as a condition for the emergence of his self. Somehow we must distinguish the inconsistency of the exploiter of inconsistencies from that of those whose inconsistencies he exploits. Perhaps we shall want to say that the inconsistency of an attacker is ontological, while other inconsistencies are logical. But it is very difficult to maintain any such distinction. For who is to say when an inconsistency may *not* be evocative of the self? The man accused *ad hominem* of harboring an inconsistency between his position and the intentions that led him to take that position might, for all we know, take the nonstandard attitude toward this contradiction. He might claim that the simultaneous endorsement of both its poles is an exercise that brings his self into focus. He may demand to know why he is any less entitled to a self than is his attacker. If he starts to argue in this way, he is engaging in a sort of counter-*argumentum ad hominem*. Its relations to the original argument that provoked it are complex to say the least. But this counter-*argumentum ad hominem* seems to be the first step into a logical pandemonium. In a moment, every argument will be allowed and no one will have the slightest hope of distinguishing the valid from the invalid. And yet this step into pandemonium seems to be clearly authorized so long as the original user of *argumentum ad hominem* is unable to explain how his ontological inconsistency differs from an ordinary logical inconsistency—and why the inconsistency of the man he attacks cannot also be ontological. I am not at all sure that this explanation is possible.

The criticisms of the thesis that philosophical positions must be attacked *ad hominem* rather than *ad rem* do not conclusively prove that this thesis is false, only that it has not yet been satisfactorily defended. There is in fact a further version of it that is sufficiently vague to be true. This is that you don't get a man to change his position in philosophy by beating him over the head with facts. You "refute" him by pointing to hard evidence, but his mind will be unchanged. Having myself often been "refuted" in this way, I would characterize it as a very confusing experience. Your interlocutor is yelling that such-and-such a fact proves you completely wrong, and insinuating that you are a fool unworthy of the attention of the roomful of people who came to hear you, but somehow you can't see where his words put pressure on your position. This situation can equally well occur when your interlocutor is poking logical holes in your position instead of hitting you over the head with facts. In other words, an argument that is intended, like an *argumentum ad hominem,* to expose an inconsistency, can also leave untouched the position it attacks. What I am trying to suggest is that there may be circumstances in which it is too much to expect strangers to engage in fruitful dialogue with one another. To argue effectively with another, one must have access to his mind. One must be able to show him in his own terms the evidential or logical rock on which his position has foundered. This demonstration requires diplomacy and patience. It might require the critic to spend his entire lifetime in the company of the man whose position he was criticizing. Perhaps not even this would be sufficient.

In any event, the intercourse between two people coming to know each other well enough for one of them to succeed in making clear to the other the limitations of his position takes the form of an *argumentum ad hominem* whether the limitations expressed are evidential or logical. The argument is addressed to the man. And the thesis that philosophical arguments are, or ought to be, *ad hominem* can certainly be maintained if *argumentum ad hominem* is taken in this vague sense. But notice a shift in perspective. Earlier I was talking about *argumentum ad hominem* as the only *valid* argument in philosophy, given the claim of each position to define what it is to be a fact. Now I am contending that *argumentum ad hominem* is the only *effective* argument in philosophy. It is thus in rhetorical terms that I am evaluating it. Not that such an argument is necessarily invalid. It may still be the case that if there is any valid philosophical argument at all, it must be this. But the validity of such arguments is not what at the moment primarily concerns us about them.

When the validity of philosophical arguments is emphasized, as opposed to their effectiveness, the distinction between logical and rhetorical success comes into focus. It is natural to suppose that an argument can be valid even when no one recognizes its validity, and that an argument can be invalid even when everyone regards it as valid. But it would be strange to suppose that an argument could be rhetorically successful even when no one acknowledged that success, or rhetorically unsuccessful even when all appearances were to the contrary. An argument is rhetorically successful when it moves people. In the very act of being moved, they at least are in effect acknowledging its success.

The distinction between the logical and rhetorical success of philosophical arguments can be elaborated into a metaphilosophical doctrine.[4] To insist on using valid philosophical arguments, as opposed to persuasive ones, is to participate in a domain of autonomous arguers. Membership in this domain is determined by whether one is arguing under the guidance of a certain Categorical Imperative; namely, "Use only those techniques of argumentation that you would be willing to allow your interlocutor to use also." This principle of bilaterality seems required if we are to specify a sense of validity relevant to philosophical arguments. We don't want to identify valid philosophical arguments with formally valid ones, because we feel that the validity of an *argumentum ad hominem* does not reside in its form. Indeed, there are reasons to suppose that no philosophical argument capable of being judged formally valid can be successful.[5] Where the validity of an *argumentum ad hominem* does seem to reside is in its fairness. It is valid because it takes the advocate of the position it attacks at his own word. In addition, it does not rule out the use of a similar argument by attackee against attacker. The Categorical Imperative I just mentioned is just a principle of fairness. If it is fair for me to use a certain argument against you, then it is fair that you should use the same argument against me.

Is what I have just said consistent with the contention that the validity of an argument is a transcendent property, a property that the argument might possess even though we failed to recognize it, or lack even though we thought the argument possessed it? If validity is in this sense transcendent, it is impossible for anyone to be sure he is carrying out the duty exacted of him by the Categorical Imperative. But this situation is cheerfully acknowledged in the ethical theory that is obviously serving as our model. "If we attend to our experience of the way men act," wrote Kant, "we meet frequent and, as we ourselves confess, justified complaints that we cannot cite a single example of the disposition to act from pure duty."[6] But examples do not *belong* to the domain governed by duty. No more do they belong to the domain of autonomous action governed by the Categorical Imperative of validity. As long as our hearts are in the right place, our conduct in arguing cannot be faulted. The Good Will "shines like a jewel by its own light," even when totally impotent.

In Kantian ethics there is of course another domain, the domain of heteronomous action. This is a domain of causal relations. The imperatives on which we act heteronomously are based on the knowledge that certain acts have certain consequences. We know, for example, that if we turn up the thermostat, the house will get warm; so if we want to get warm, we turn up the thermostat. Heteronomous acts are those having their origin in conditions outside the agent's own self-legislating moral deliberations. In this case causality is brought to bear on the transaction through the agent's knowledge of the conditions that will produce the result he desires. In other cases causality can more directly control the agent's behavior, as when he is subject to manipulation. It is perhaps in this case that his action is most clearly heteronomous.

If we want to find argumentation occurring within a heteronomous domain, we do not have far to look. Rhetoric relies on causal connections. A speaker has purposes, which he attempts to carry out by making use of these connections. He is thus behaving heteronomously. His heteronomous behavior, furthermore, consists in dealing with his audience on the assumption that it, too, behaves heteronomously; he manipulates it. The cardinal principle he must espouse is that of unilaterality: "Try to prevent your audience from using against you the techniques of argumentation you use against it." Contrast this with the principle of bilaterality used by the philosophical arguer: "Use only those techniques of argumentation that you would be willing to allow your interlocutor to use also." The critic welcomes the chance to be criticized in turn, but the manipulator cannot afford to be manipulated.

Rhetorical success is not transcendent. It belongs to the realm of nature, to what Kant called the phenomenal world. We can give examples of rhetorical success, even if we cannot exemplify valid philosophical arguments.

By now it is clear that our initial characterization of philosophy has presupposed a view of the nature of rhetoric. If a philosophy is an attempt to define what it is to be a fact, then communication across the intergalactic spaces separating philosophical positions is possible only via *argumentum ad hominem*. If *argumentum ad hominem* is to be valid, it must answer to the imperative of bilaterality. No place is left for the unilateral enterprise that comes to be thought of as rhetoric.

At this point we begin our trip through the land of Rhetoric. We are escorted on our way by questions such as: Is rhetoric *necessarily* unilateral and manipulative? Can there be no bilateral rhetoric? Are we satisfied on other counts with the characterization of rhetoric that has emerged? Are we sure we want to say that there is no aspect or example of philosophical argumentation that we would be willing to see characterized as rhetorical?

Part of what we are inclined to say in reply stems from what we might claim is a more adequate conception of the nature of rhetoric, and part from observation of the actual practices of philosophical argumentation. Notice that the acceptance of evidence of this second kind already marks a departure from our initial position. If a philosophy defines what it is to be a fact, then even the facts about philosophical argumentation itself will not be philosophically neutral. A truly rigorous defender of the position concerning the nature of philosophy that we have outlined would reject any alleged counter-evidence concerning the nature of philosophy—including "evidence" of a rhetorical vector in philosophical argumentation—as question-begging. So if this evidence is admitted, he has let down his guard. What caused him to do that? Perhaps nothing more than the desire to talk to someone else.

First, however, let us consider whether the characterization of rhetoric as manipulative is adequate. One cue is that the phrase "manipulative rhetoric" does not strike us as redundant. But if rhetoric were necessarily manipulative, as squares are necessarily rectangular, then "manipulative rhetoric" would be as much a pleonasm as "rectangular square." Yet surely not all rhetoric is manipulative. We want to contrast the manipulative rhetoric of the demagogue or confidence man with the nonmanipulative rhetoric of the diplomat or ironist. Hitler no doubt engaged in manipulative rhetoric, but he was not the only speaker who ever lived. If we want to say that Hitler's rhetoric was evil because manipulative, then we have to be prepared to admit that a good rhetoric that does not manipulate is at least possible.

Consider also whether it is really accurate to characterize all rhetoric as unilateral. I have mentioned the diplomat. If he conceals from his interlocutors any of the argumentative techniques he is using, he is sure to be found out sooner or later, and the agreement he has secured will come unstuck. He ought to welcome the use against his own position of precisely those techniques he is himself using, for only in such use can the degree to which all the parties to the discussion understand each other be tested. Unilateral rhetoric no doubt has its place in human affairs, but it is useful primarily in short-term situations in which the rhetor is trying to get his audience to take an irrevocable step and is not concerned with its opinion of him once it finds out what he has been up to. Settlements that have to be negotiated and ratified, however, require a bilateral rhetoric.

It might be contended that even if not all rhetoric is unilateral, still the unilateral is a very important kind, in that the adversary system of justice depends upon the unilateral presentation of one's own case. This contention is really irrelevant, because as long as it is admitted that at least *some* rhetoric is bilateral, it follows that the Kant-like distinction between rhetoric and philosophical argumentation is a distortion. But I bring the point up partly to sharpen the conception of unilaterality. For the adversary system does not really depend on a unilateral rhetoric at all. The defendent at a trial is not trying to prevent the prosecution from using the same *techniques of argumentation* that he uses. He is simply using techniques of argumentation open to all in the courtroom to present his version of the truth. This version may be slanted, but the judge would soon put an end to any effort on his part to use unfair tactics to get it across. Unilateral techniques are ruled out as "irrelevant, incompetent, and immaterial."

If one is told that rhetoric is a set of techniques making use of causal connections, then one gets the impression that we could waive its use, as we waive the use of any other art. Just as the hunter can lay aside his spear and the potter his wheel, so the speaker can lay aside his use of rhetoric. But is this really possible? How would one go about refraining from rhetoric? Clearly it is not enough to refrain from speech; for silence has a rhetorical function. Should the person seeking to abstain from rhetoric, then, leave his community and live in solitude? Already we see how very much more he is asking of himself than does the hunter who wishes to give up hunting for a time. But it is still not enough. For the process through which a person gets *himself* to act or to accept certain conclusions is also rhetorical. There is no difference in principle between self-persuasion and the persuasion of others.[7] And yet it is clear that one who gave up persuading himself would be giving up his humanity. Like a beast, he would lack the power of deliberation.

To be human, then, is to practice rhetoric. But we cannot say that to be human is to practice any particular art based on a knowledge of causal connections. Hence rhetoric is not a particular art based on a knowledge of causal connections, and any account of the relation between rhetoric and philosophical argumentation that represents it in this way misrepresents it.

There are other arguments as well for the necessity of rhetoric to human life and its ubiquity in experience. One of them depends on the consideration that to be conscious, a person must be able to distinguish himself from the data he receives.[8] A machine cannot in principle be distinguished from its input; the signals fed into it are elements of a continuous system. For this reason, a machine cannot be said to be conscious of its input. No more are humans conscious of the input to their sense-organs and brain. Only when a wedge has been driven between the person and the data he receives can he be said to be conscious of these data. He then stands apart from the data; he pays attention to them. By what means do we secure this attention? It has long been acknowledged that one person can use rhetoric to call the attention of another to conditions of which he had been unconscious. It is no more than a natural extension of the use of the term to apply it to situations in which the person makes himself attend to data. This reflexive rhetoric must occur wherever consciousness occurs. If philosophers are conscious, they must engage in rhetoric that is at least self-directed.[9]

Of course it can be argued that even though man is by nature a rhetorical animal, his arguments over philosophical issues need not be judged in rhetorical terms. For what we want to know about a philosophical argument is not whether it is rhetorically successful or not, but whether it is logically successful, i.e., valid.[10] Yet in view of the distinction between good and evil rhetoric, it is difficult to maintain that rhetorical considerations are irrelevant to the evaluation of philosophical argumentation. Surely not all use of rhetoric by arguing philosophers is of the evil sort. Some of it must be good. But what do we mean by "a good rhetoric"? We do not mean a *successful* rhetoric, since an evil rhetoric can also be successful. We mean something more like a *nonmanipulative,* a *bilateral* rhetoric. But how are we to distinguish this rhetoric from valid philosophical argumentation, since the only criterion for the validity of the latter seems to be its bilaterality? Precisely the considerations that would have led us to say that the argument was rhetorically beyond reproach also lead us to say that it is logically successful.

But it is not maximally convincing to argue merely that it would be strange if there were no philosophical arguments exhibiting good rhetoric. Strange situations do occur. The time has come to give examples of the rhetoric of philosophers and to consider how this rhetoric is related to the validity of their arguments. It has been pointed out, for instance, that the Wittgenstein of the *Tractatus* was engaged in elucidation and that Heidegger's mission in *Being and Time* was evocative.[11] Elucidation is the process of clarifying propositions. This process is obviously different from that of either *transmitting* or *proving* propositions. ("Philosophy does not result in 'philosophical propositions,' but rather in the clarification of propositions."[12]) Nor is clarification, in Wittgenstein's sense, a matter of formulating propositions more precisely. Clarification of a sort may result from the increase of precision, but this is not the kind of clarification Wittgenstein had in mind. He wanted his propositions to be luminous, not precise. But it is a function of rhetoric, the art of presentation, to render propositions luminous. And there is no reason why this rhetoric should not be bilateral. Indeed, it would be ridiculous to suppose that Wittgenstein was using concealed techniques here (what would that mean?) or that he would not himself have been open to someone else's presentation of the very sort of elucidation that he was trying to provide.

Suppose we try to distinguish Wittgenstein's argumentation in the *Tractatus* from his rhetoric. This will not be easy. He is asking us to see things in a new way, to find luminous propositions which previously had been opaque to us. Such elucidation could be the office of argumentation as well as of rhetoric.

With Heidegger, the case is even simpler. Evocation—the awakening of readers to a forgotten truth—is clearly a rhetorical achievement. And there is no reason to suppose that the rhetoric involved is not bilateral. Whatever Heidegger may be like as a concrete person, there is no reason in principle why he should refuse to listen to arguments based on the same techniques he has used. This is, furthermore, a case in which it would be extremely difficult to distinguish argumentation and rhetoric.

I do not want to leave the impression, however, that I regard Wittgenstein and Heidegger as the only two philosophers in whose writings argumentation and a good rhetoric have coincided. It would be hard to think of a major figure in the literature of whom this is *not* true. Consider the phrase "The Rhetoric of _____," and put the name of any major figure in the blank. We can at least make sense of the project that would be required if the resulting phrase were to be the title of an assigned paper. Plato would be very easy to deal with, but even Descartes and Spinoza would not be hard. There would even be a point in talking about the rhetoric of W. V. Quine. And in each case, we would have trouble distinguishing the rhetoric of the man from his argumentation, or the success of his rhetoric from the validity of his argumentation. Of course if validity is formal validity, we can make the distinction. But I have been contending that the validity of a philosophical argument is determined by considerations other than formal structure.

Even if we cannot distinguish the logical success of a philosophical argument from its rhetorical success, we might persist in maintaining that philosophy is a rational enterprise, hence that the discourse of philosophers is opaque to analysis in exclusively rhetorical terms. Yet when we try to isolate the peculiarly rational aspect of this discourse, we seem to be forced to locate it in the activity of criticism.[13] And philosophical criticism is inherently negative, destructive of the claims it examines. Nor is the critical act itself immune to criticism. Nothing in philosophical discourse seems to have any ultimate logical footing. (If there are logical successes, they are, like most successes, transient episodes.) Hence logic is not the most promising category in which to attempt to account for the rationality of the philosophical enterprise. Rhetoric is in fact more promising. For when a critic destroys an opposing claim, the rhetorical work he has done is more important than the logical. Even though his criticism may not in the last analysis be tenable, it has inflicted lasting damage, awakening suspicions that cannot thenceforth be put to rest. It is not totally perverse to say that philosophy is rational precisely insofar as philosophers are rendered suspicious of each other's claims.

We have traveled from philosophy through rhetoric; i.e., from an initial conception of the nature of philosophy to the conception of rhetoric that seems to be entailed by it, and thence through a revision of this latter conception that seems to be dictated by its inadequacies and limitations. We stand now in a position in which we see rhetoric from a new perspective. How does philosophy now look from this perspective? There have already been intimations of its new appearance. Our trip back to philosophy will confirm and systematize these intimations. Now instead of eliciting the view of rhetoric presupposed by an initial view of philosophy, we elicit a view of philosophy presupposed by a more developed view of rhetoric.

The initial view presupposed a dualism. It asserted the independent existence of two worlds: the world of autonomous action and that of heteronomous action. Valid philosophical argumentation was alleged to belong to the former, and rhetoric to the latter. Rhetorical success depends on the laws of nature, and can be observed whenever a speaker uses his knowledge of causal connections to get an audience or an interlocutor to do what he wants it to do or to adopt the beliefs he wants it to adopt. Logical success, on the other hand, is not the sort of condition we can ever be sure of observing. It belongs to the noumenal world and is, like the Good Will, transcendent. The law governing logical success is the Categorical Imperative of bilaterality. This contrasts with the law governing rhetorical success; i.e., the Hypothetical Imperative of unilaterality. Finally, we can contrast imperatives of these two kinds by saying that only the former defines a world of rational beings. To be rational, it is necessary to participate in a world governed by the principle of bilaterality. We affirm our own rationality by affirming that of others. But it is not necessary to man as such or to any other rational being that he act on the basis of the hypothetical imperatives of rhetoric.

We have in effect been attacking this dualism. To take up the last point first, we saw that one cannot write off rhetoric as unnecessary to human life. Nor is the necessity purely biological. To be rational, any being would require at least a reflexive rhetoric, because rationality requires at least attention to data. Also, rationality presupposes deliberation, which again presupposes a self-directed rhetoric.

We have also seen that rhetoric is not necessarily unilateral. Perhaps it is unilateral only when it is manipulative. In any event, there is no reason why a bilateral argument cannot have a rhetorical vector.

What is on the rhetorical side of the alleged chasm, then, seems to be invading the side reserved for philosophical argumentation. At the same time we have seen how very much more rhetorical philosophical argumentation is than it had at first seemed to be. Not only does it perform functions such as evocation that we might naturally expect of rhetoric, but in a more general way philosophical argumentation embodies the rhetoric inextricably in all discourse.

I mentioned the rhetoric of Plato, Descartes, Spinoza, and Quine, exemplifying ways in which we might fill in the blank in the expression "The Rhetoric of _____." Of course the result of filling in the blank could be used pejoratively. Someone might talk about the rhetoric of Plato in order to distinguish this aspect of Plato's writing from a more responsible, less questionable aspect either in Plato's writings or in those of someone else. No doubt some parts of the Platonic corpus and the writings of some philosophers other than Plato are more responsible and less questionable than certain Platonic writings. But do we really want to withhold the term "rhetorical" from the more acceptable parts? Even the most responsible and least questionable philosophical writings that there are have a rhetorical vector. It is this vector that renders them more than just collections of principles or evidence. For the way a philosopher *presents* his principles or evidence is essential to the intelligibility of his position. A bare outline of a thinker's doctrines, ripped out of its rhetorical context, is intelligible only to a person who can picture that context. Books in the College Outline Series are not noted for their capacity to teach philosophy. We cannot hope to understand Plato unless we are acquainted with the dialogic form in which Plato expressed himself, and we will have serious difficulties with Spinoza if we try to dissociate his doctrines from his geometrical presentation of them.

It may seem that my case depends on the unexamined assumption that rhetoric is the art of presentation. What if it were instead to be construed as the art of persuasion? Could we not then clearly distinguish, for example, the places in Plato where he is trying to persuade us even against our better judgment and those in which he simply points to the truth, leaving it up to us to decide whether to be persuaded or not? We might attempt to make such a distinction, but it would not be a clear-cut one. It is never the case that Plato, or any other thinker, simply places the truth before us and lets us decide. The very act of bringing us into confrontation with the truth is tendentious. Even the biblical injunction "They who have ears, let them hear" is intended to be a step toward persuasion.

Suppose, then, that a case has been made out for regarding even the most responsible and least questionable philosophical statements as rhetorical, whether rhetoric is construed as presentation, or persuasion, or anything else. The question then arises: "How do you distinguish philosophical discourse from discourse of any other kind, e.g., scientific? For clearly the scientist too aims to present, persuade, etc."

The answer, I think, is at least partly that distinct philosophies involve distinct rhetorics, while the scientific enterprise makes use of a single rhetoric—the rhetoric of the research paper—which comes close to being a rhetoric of objective fact. In other words, there is a single rhetoric the scientist uses to call our attention to his results—to evoke consciousness. What he calls our attention to, furthermore, is a truth outside the rhetorical process—a truth which he thinks would continue to be available even if communicated to no one. Rhetoric is important to the scientist only insofar as he is a member of a community of inquirers, academic or other. It plays no part, however—at least so we are led to suppose—in his investigations themselves.

In philosophy, on the other hand, each investigation has a distinctive rhetoric, which is necessary in the sense that in its absence there would be no truths at all. Rhetoric is discovery as well as presentation or persuasion. The philosopher does not just stumble on truths; he reaches them through argumentation. What does it mean, for example, to say that there are universals if we cannot produce the arguments? But argumentation and rhetoric converge in philosophy. Argumentation is the art of presenting philosophical conclusions so that they are plausible. Without it, they would not even be intelligible. What is one to make of the bare statement "There are universals" when it is not embedded in an argumentative context? The thesis must be properly presented before we can deal with it. Some effort must have been made to persuade us of its truth.

But representatives of different schools of philosophy have used different styles of argumentation to present their conclusions. Consider the arguments of Descartes and Locke. The former bespeak an implicit trust in reason; the latter are more cautious and evidential. Instead of arguing a priori from the *cogito* to the existence of innate ideas in general, as Descartes does, Locke attacks the doctrine of innate ideas on the ground that he can find no examples of any. Two rhetorics are at work here—the rhetoric of rationalism and that of empiricism.

My contention, then, is that each major philosophical position has its own style of rhetoric, and the style is integral to the position. This contention contrasts with the initial view that philosophical positions are monadistically isolated attempts to define what it is to be a fact and that in the face of this monadistic isolation only a bilateral and nonrhetorical form of argumentation offers any hope. One important difference arises from the fact that the use of rhetoric implies the existence of an audience. Philosophies, in other words, necessarily have audiences; the question whether they are systematically cut off from all except those who obviously share the same definition of what it is to be a fact does not arise.

If differing metaphysical positions are not monadistically isolated from one another, how *are* they related? The fact that they can hold the attention of a common audience should tell us something about their relationship. Each of the rival positions is an articulation of what the audience grasps but does not articulate—what Hegel called "The Idea," what might also be called The Whole. The arguments for each position appeal, at least implicitly, to this vision of a totality potentially available to all. Much though the positions clash, much though their supporting rhetorics collide, each has a part to play in the dialectical advance which either ideally terminates, or will someday actually terminate, in the final articulation of The Whole.

So the gulf separating metaphysical positions turns out to be unreal. Another gulf that we have in effect denied by refusing to separate a position from its rhetoric is that between the realm of heteronomy and the realm of autonomy—between Nature and Reason. We are now thinking of philosophical reason as existing only concretely—as requiring rhetorical articulation by speakers facing audiences. (Of course in using the words "speaker" and "audience" I do not mean to be giving short shrift to the written word.) This is not to say, however, that philosophical reason has fallen into a heteronomous domain. We cannot plot or predict the exact effect of our philosophical rhetoric. It may fall on deaf ears or receptive ones. Causal knowledge is not much of a help. What is more helpful is historical knowledge, in the sense of sensitivity to the results of asking whether the ideas one is proposing are ideas whose time has come.

In the midworld of history, halfway between pure autonomy and pure heteronomy, reason and rhetoric are inextricably fused. If it is Kantian to separate the world of nature and that of reason, it is Hegelian to insist on the fusion. Hegel felt that the Categorical Imperative is best exemplified in the institutions of one's own culture. He might also have felt—I do not have any conclusive evidence of this—that philosophical reasoning is best exemplified by the philosophical rhetoric of a particular era.

Let me try to exemplify how a philosophical position articulates The Whole and how the gulf between Nature and Reason is overcome. I borrow my example from Hegel himself—the Being-Nothing sequence in the Shorter Logic. (I leave aside Becoming, the dialectical synthesis of Being and Nothing.) "Pure Being makes the beginning," says Hegel, "because it is on the one hand pure thought and on the other immediacy itself, simple and indeterminate; and the first beginning cannot be mediated by anything, or be further determined."[14] As an example of a philosophy of Being, Hegel cites the view of Parmenides. The rhetoric of Being is a rhetoric of absolute certainty. Uncertainty may attend statements asserting the existence of particular things, but not that of Being itself. Being is, and nonbeing is not. Here, it might seem, is ontological bedrock.

To quote Hegel, however, "This mere Being, as it is mere abstraction, is therefore the absolutely negative: which, in a similarly immediate aspect, is just Nothing."[15] The philosophy of Nothing is illustrated by Buddhism, and the rhetoric of Nothing is a polemical rhetoric, which attacks all notions of the existence of a non-null absolute. "Not this, not that" is the characteristic pattern of this rhetoric. It attacks the absolute certainty characteristic of the rhetoric of Being.

Both the metaphysics of Being and that of Nothing are very early attempts—early at least in the Hegelian system—to articulate The Whole. It is only because they share this project that they are both capable of appealing to the same audience—an audience that might be conveniently defined as the readership of the Shorter Logic. What, now, are we to make of the polemic that the advocate of Nothing addresses to the advocate of Being? Will this polemic constitute a counter-example to the thesis that all valid argumentation in philosophy is *ad hominem*? Does it appeal to the intentions of the supporter of Being, or does it rather appeal to what everyone in the audience knows? If the latter, it is *ad rem*. But in fact no appeal *is* made, either here or at any other juncture of the Hegelian dialectic, to what everyone knows, to the common but unarticulated vision of The Whole. The argument in this case is that it is the very intentions of the supporter of Being that turn him into a supporter of Nothing. Nor is consistency the issue here; the Ontist is not turned into a Nihilist by virtue of considerations of consistency, but expresses Nihilist principles in the very effort to express Ontist principles. *Argumentum ad hominem* as previously envisaged essentially required a dialogue; e.g., between Bergson's critic and Bergson. But what we now have in mind is the result of a monologue, the talk Spirit engages in to develop itself.

An important question remains. *Even if* I have now made it seem plausible that various philosophies have various rhetorics, while there is only one rhetoric of science, it might be objected that I have not yet sufficiently delimited philosophy. For in modes of discourse aside from both philosophy and science, there might also be a variety of rhetorical styles. One could think of politics in this way, for example. There is a rhetoric of conservatism and one of liberalism. There are two ways of reacting to this challenge. One is to argue that liberalism and conservatism are themselves philosophies, and that any discourse with a distinctive rhetoric would be a philosophy. But I don't know whether this answer can ultimately be defended. Perhaps it is better to fall back on the other alternative and say that it was not my purpose in this paper to give an exhaustive characterization of philosophy, only to show how certain ideas about it undergo change as the result of a journey through the domain of rhetoric.

Rhetoric and Public Knowledge

Lloyd F. Bitzer

I wish to express appreciation to the Department of Communication and Purdue University for making possible my visit here, and to Carol Jablonski and Professor Don Burks for their generous introductory remarks. I am delighted to take part in this program, which brings me into the company of scholars I have admired for many years. With each I have enjoyed a valued personal relationship, and to each I am indebted. Donald Bryant taught me rhetoric and directed my studies at the University of Iowa. Maurice Natanson taught me philosophy at the University of North Carolina. Wayne Booth participated in the National Developmental Project on Rhetoric, which I helped direct. Henry Johnstone's friendship and good counsel I have appreciated since we first met in 1963. I came to know Kenneth Burke when he visited the University of Wisconsin in 1969 to address our seminars. Burke's influence on rhetoric and literature need not be underscored here; but I would share with you a clue to the humanity of the man, expressed eloquently in a letter I treasure. After Burke's Wisconsin visit, I wrote to him, thanking him for contributing to our intellectual life and noting the strong influence he has made on rhetorical studies. My letter accompanied him to Europe. From Venice he responded on June 20, 1969:

> This is to thank you most gratefully for your generous letter, which reached me just when I was preparing to leave for a brief trip to Europe. A death in the family made kind words doubly welcome. I came to southern France, to attend a conference, and am extending my trip somewhat, for distraction.
>
> It was good of you to write. I am always in sickly need of reassurance!

"In sickly need of reassurance"—a poignant confession of a man who has opened perspectives on the universe of ideas and toiled relentlessly, sometimes alone, in the search. His words announce the ache of many kindred minds.

This reflection on Burke provides an opening to my subject, which deals with communities of persons who share ideas, sentiments, feelings, and purposes, and who may be said to need reassurance that their thoughts and actions are authorized.

The questions I shall ask in this essay are: What is a public? What is public knowledge? What is the relationship between rhetoric and public knowledge? In response I shall suggest that:

A public is a community of persons who share conceptions, principles, interests, and values, and who are significantly interdependent. This community may be characterized further by institutions such as offices, schools, laws, tribunals; by a duration sufficient to the development of these institutions; by a commitment to the well-being of members; and by a power of authorization through which some truths and values are accredited.

Public knowledge I understand to be a kind of knowledge needful to public life and actually present somewhat to all who dwell in community. Public knowledge differs from private knowledge, from private knowledge made generally available, and from mere public opinion. It may be regarded as a fund of truths, principles, and values which could only characterize a public. A public in possession of such knowledge is made competent to accredit new truth and value and to authorize decision and action.

Rhetoric is a method of inquiry and communication which seeks to establish correct judgments, primarily in the areas of practical and humane affairs, for the speaker or writer and for the audience addressed. With respect to public knowledge, rhetoric generates truths and values previously unknown to a public, gives voice to interests and principles whose locus is a public, serves as an instrument with which to test public truths and values and to select and justify public means and ends. In general, rhetoric at its best sustains wisdom in the life of a public.

1

Theories of rhetoric conceived as stylistics, or as the psychology of language and symbolic behavior, or as propaganda, do not require a conception of the public. Such theories do need a notion of audience—a class of persons whose cognitive and affective states and whose habits of thought and language must be understood by a communicator who would inform or persuade effectively. The notion of the public also will be subordinate or unimportant in rhetorics which find grounds of knowledge and action in revelation, in some ideal realm apart from human experience, or in the encounter of a single mind with external reality: when, in other words, knowledge can be obtained in the absence of any public. A notion of the public will be essential, however, to any theory of rhetoric that regards collective human experience as the legitimate source of some truths and, thus, the authoritative ground of a class of decisions and actions. Some organization of persons—some public— must function as the source or carrier of truths and values thought to be indispensable. To clarify and explore the conception of the public is the main purpose of this essay.

There is an ancient quarrel between rhetoric and philosophy, stretching from the pre-Socratics to the present. Plato dramatized the quarrel in his dialogue *Gorgias:* he likened rhetoric to cookery and declared there is no genuine art of rhetoric, if rhetoric is conceived in terms promulgated by the sophistic teachers. The quarrel persisted throughout antiquity; evidence of its history and continuation are found in Cicero's works on rhetoric, in the second book of Quintilian's *Institutes,* in the *Rhetoric* of Philodemus, in the attack on all rhetorics by the skeptic Sextus Empiricus, and in numerous other writers. After the classical period, the issues in the dispute turned chiefly on the themes Plato had set: whether rhetoric is founded upon and expressive of truth, and whether rhetoric's products are valuable. There is no genuine art of rhetoric, said Plato in the *Phaedrus,* except one founded upon high speculation regarding the great truths of nature and human nature, and there is no true rhetoric unless its outcomes are valuable. Wisdom, Plato insisted again and again, is the foundation of a true art of rhetoric.

Might the knowledge sufficient for a true art of rhetoric reside somehow in the public, or in publics? One conception of public knowledge Plato entertained and rejected in the *Gorgias.* Socrates tells his interlocutor, Callicles, that public opinion, which is the "love" of Callicles, is unstable and unreliable.

> I perceive that you and I have a common feeling. For we are lovers both, and both of us have two loves apiece:—I am the lover of Alcibiades, the son of Cleinias, and of philosophy; and you of the Athenian Demus, and of Demus the son of Pyrilampes. Now, I observe that you, with all your cleverness, do not venture to contradict your favourite in any word or opinion of his; but as he changes you change, backwards and forwards. When the Athenian Demus denies anything that you are saying in the assembly, you go over to his opinion; and you do the same with Demus, the fair young son of Pyrilampes. For you have not the power to resist the words and ideas of your loves; and if a person were to express surprise at the strangeness of what you say from time to time when under their influence, you would probably reply to him, if you were honest, that you cannot help saying what your loves say unless they are prevented; and that you can only be silent when they are. Now you must understand that my words are an echo too, and therefore you need not wonder at me; but if you want to silence me, silence philosophy, who is my love, for she is always telling me what I am now telling you, my friend; neither is she capricious like my other love, for

> the son of Cleinias says one thing to-day and another thing to-morrow, but philosophy is always true. She is the teacher at whose words you are now wondering, and you have heard her yourself. Her you must refute. . . .[1]

Clearly, Plato here discredits shallow public opinion, blown this way and that by winds of fashion. Philosophical wisdom, steady and true, is his sure ground of political discourse.

While Plato rejects public opinion as the ground of discourse and action in the service of the public, he does not discount the possibility that somehow a community, or some part of it, may possess wisdom and carry it forward in its literature, tradition, and education. The myth which concludes his *Phaedrus* warns us against forgetfulness; perhaps Plato implies there is a wisdom, an accumulated knowledge, entrusted to or generated by a culture, which must be preserved and rehearsed, as well as tested and perfected, lest it be forgotten.

We need not explore Plato's position further, since the quarrel is clear: the issue is between shifting or unreliable public opinion on the one hand, and knowledge on the other. If we agree that knowledge is necessary to proper rhetorical practice and if we admit that knowledge of some kind might be discovered or made, and in any case authorized by communities or publics, then we are led to inquire about the existence, nature, quality, and foundation of this knowledge.

Attention to the public, or publics, can be justified on a different theoretical interest. As we are interested in the notions of speaker, audience, and message, so we are interested also in formulating a precise understanding of the public, for the public is a familiar term in association with rhetoric. We teach public communication; we engage in public discussion and debate; as citizens, we are concerned about the public interest; as rhetoricians, we explore the nature of public discourse, which involves such matters as the public interest, public issues, and persons in their public rather than private characters. Thus we have cause to ask, What is this "public" which figures so prominently in discussions of rhetorical theory and practice and of political systems? How does the public differ, if at all, from the audience or from a collection of citizens?

We may be puzzled also by the fact that while the public is an important notion in numerous rhetorics, it is obscure or nonexistent in others. Aristotle's *Rhetoric* presumes a public whose conceptions of the good are represented by participants in deliberative, forensic, and epideictic situations, and whose wisdom supplies premises of rhetorical discourse. Quintilian's statesman-orator attends both to the case at hand and to the interests of the public, and in duty to real public interest, this orator may sometimes justly deceive his audience. These and many other theorists, who place rhetoric in settings mainly civic, establish rather clear ties between rhetoric and political publics. On the other hand, the rhetorics of Saint Augustine, Campbell, Whately, Bain, Chaim Perelman, and Kenneth Burke do not establish clear ties with political publics. In some of these, however, a notion rather like the public may be observed: for example, Perelman's "universal audience" appears to be a kind of public, but not political. The scientific rhetorics of the eighteenth and nineteenth centuries could easily dispense with the notion of publics, since the ground of truthful expression was thought to depend on the contact of individual minds with intuitively certain data; and such theories accounted for communities, or societies of persons united in sentiment, by reference to principles and mechanisms of human nature, among which "sympathy" played a leading part.

Practical motives, as well as theoretical, underlie this study. We suspect, perhaps, that contemporary publics are in disarray, unable to give expression to truths and impulses essential to high achievement. Is it possible that publics need to be identified anew, reinforced, endowed with a knowledge directive of growth toward civilization? We observe communities engaged in exceedingly dangerous competitions and are led to inquire whether there can be found a wisdom conducive to harmony.

Furthermore, ours may be a time of transition from local and national publics to more universal ones. If so, what would be the features of a universal or international public? The conditions of its orderly growth? What truths, values, and principles would characterize it? Over a great part of human history, publics were formed within geographical contexts, constrained by seas, mountains, and other borders. They were rhetorical in the sense that communication carried forward their traditions and was instrumental in various ways to their lives. Today, however, publics are rhetorical in a different manner. They are carved out less by exigencies in local geographical contexts and more by communications which shape consciousness and call attention to massive problems which cross traditional political boundaries and are essentially universal. Thus, the possible existence of a universal political public which might become self-conscious and articulate must be acknowledged.

2

The argument to be developed in this section proceeds in four stages: to establish, first, that rhetoric requires connection with knowledge of some sort; second, that public rhetorical discourse is representational in the sense that speakers and audiences "stand in for" the public; third, that such representation is competent insofar as the agent knows what the public knows; and fourth, that whatever is said or done in the public's behalf needs authorization.

First, people routinely distinguish between the true and the false, between claims indisputable and disputable, between knowledge and opinion, between correct and incorrect methods of inquiry and confirmation, and among kinds of knowledge and degrees of certainty. That such distinctions are employed in the sciences, arts, and in many kinds of practical deliberation is beyond contention. It is also an observable fact that people frequently select knowledge over opinion, deliberate successfully about matters of truth and value, and assert to be true and valuable what actually is true and valuable. Whoever would deny these propositions is obliged to assert a position counter to observable facts and intolerably self-inconsistent as well, for what he elects to deny will be affirmed both in his justifications and in his ordinary behavior. The distinction between knowledge and opinion, or between truth and mere belief is, therefore, fundamental and real. The various ways to reduce knowledge to opinion and to formulate degrees of probable knowledge alter the terms of the distinction but not its substance.

An earnest affirmation of Plato's view that rhetoric must be founded in and expressive of knowledge makes no departure from the thought of rhetoricians and philosophers who have written seriously about the nature and function of rhetoric. While offering different analyses of knowledge, assigning inquiry and confirmation to rhetoric or to other disciplines, rhetoricians and philosophers have held—I think without exception—that rhetoric needs connection with knowledge. Whether rhetoric's central field of application was thought to be politics, religion, science, artistic communication, or argumentation regarding contingent matters, theorists have regarded the art as more or less excellent insofar as it has command of knowledge. We may recall Sidney's response to the charge that poetry is "the mother of lies." In his *Defense of Poesie*, 1583, he said, "But truly I think . . . that of all writers under the sun the poet can scarcely be a liar." To lie, he said, is "to affirm that to be true which is false." But the poet, "he nothing affirms and therefore never lieth." Although the poet "recount things not true, yet because he telleth them not for true, he lieth not." No major rhetorician has offered the same defense of rhetoric—that rhetors affirm not, hence "lieth not"—and for good reason. Rhetorical discourse typically asserts that something is or is not the case, is or is not to be valued. Rhetors make claims, they often believe the claims to be true, and they seek to establish claims upon grounds thought to be true and unassailable. In argumentation related to routine affairs and to matters of civic or scholarly importance, we ourselves distinguish on some grounds between that which qualifies as knowledge and that which is to be regarded as mere opinion. Furthermore, we believe our rhetoric to be the more excellent to the extent that it is grounded in and generative of knowledge.

Second, having affirmed that rhetoric is assertive of what is thought to be true and valuable and thus needs connection with knowledge of some sort, we next observe that *public* rhetorical discourse is representational as well. This means that public speakers and audiences serve, or stand in for, publics. We often say that a person speaks for someone else, or for a group or community: an eminent scientist, in a symposium of persons representing different fields, speaks for science; an attorney represents the interests of his client; at the bargaining table, the labor leader represents members of his union. In these and many similar instances, persons represent others by means of discourse and action. Journalists affirm that their task is to serve the public by conveying valuable information; elected officials are "representatives"; social critics, political speakers, ordinary citizens, service organizations—all, from time to time, purport to represent the public. And all are thought to err or fail in duty if they present falsehood in the place of truth or if they speak or act for themselves rather than for the public they represent.

An audience is likewise representational whenever it stands in for a public. For this reason, the notion of the public must be distinguished from that of the audience. A rhetorical audience consists of persons who have the capacity to mediate change so as to modify positively the exigencies in rhetorical situations. The public must be conceived to be a different thing from an audience; for, while in some cases audience and public may overlap or coincide, in most cases they do not. For example, the Senate deliberates and acts in the interests of a public thought to consist of the citizens of the country. Obviously the Senate is not identical with the citizenry— the public whose interests are to be cared for. What is more, many senators may hold principles and interests opposed to those held by the public they represent. The Senate, as a rhetorical audience, is addressed because it has the capacity to mediate change, but it may lack the power to authorize change, whereas on the other hand the public, which in principle has the power to authorize change, may lack the capacity to mediate change.

We note incidentally that the Senate is a formally legitimate public body, since it exists by authority of, and deliberates and acts on grounds presumably authorized by, the citizenry. Such formal legitimacy is not conferred on all persons. Yet, from time to time all of us serve as public audiences and speakers; although not given formal authority by the public, we nevertheless deliberate and act in its behalf—and apparently with propriety when we represent it competently. Thus, rhetorical practice is often representational, with speakers and audiences often representing the public. We may reasonably hold that public rhetoric is *public* just because it has this representational property.

Third, how is it that one person could properly stand in for, or represent, the public? It is not because that person declares himself to be a spokesman. We know that many such declarations are counterfeit: for example, a self-proclaimed spokesman who purports to represent the public but instead serves private or special interests. Nor is it sufficient to say that anyone formally commissioned is thereby entitled to represent the public: the public sometimes disavows the words and actions of elected officials, and occasionally disqualifies officials. Nor can we answer that anyone who holds membership in a public will by virtue of membership represent it properly. A member may be ignorant of the public's interests and truths, and inarticulate as well. We may suppose that a person is entitled to speak for science if he knows and is capable of expressing the knowledge and interests of the scientific community. We may suppose also that one who rightly represents the public will know what the public knows and speak as the public would speak were it articulate and aware of its truths and interests.

In principle, a spokesman for the public possesses and employs as premises of discourse those truths, values, interests, and principles located in the public's tradition and experience—wisdom authorized or warranted by the public and part of the public domain. In a community holding near absolute uniformity of truth and interest, spokesmen would be of one voice; in a community exhibiting diversity within unity, we would expect competing voices because truths and interests will be in contention. In any case, the spokesman engages the public's fund of knowledge; his speeches echo its terms and maxims; he honors its heroes, rehearses its traditions, performs its rituals; he represents the public both to itself and to others. He does so, in many instances, not with pretense or irony, but with sincerity because he is immersed himself in the tradition and experience of his public. In his representations, he announces at times what is as yet unsaid. The "characteristic great man of our times," writes Paul Weiss, is a Gandhi or a Schweitzer who "points a people toward civilization. He defines the tone of the culture as that which is to be superseded by a civilized whole of which the culture is an anticipatory fragmentary case." The spokesman for a public—poet, statesman, leader—is rather "like a prophet in that he is a vehicle for the expression of some truth or value of importance for the people."[2]

If, as we suppose, a public consists of persons united in interests, aspirations, tradition, and experience, then anyone truly representing a public—that is, announcing its truths and interests or deliberating, judging, or acting in its behalf—must be capable of rich sympathetic understanding and feeling which virtually unites him with that public. Moreover, he needs to possess the knowledge and interests of his public. Without these things, he lacks competence and, thus, is not authorized to speak or act.

Fourth, authorization, entitlement, accreditation are terms that figure large in this discussion and require clarification. What, we may ask, is the authority for what we say and do? A man about to fell a tree might ask: Who or what agency or principle authorizes this act? A military officer about to order soldiers to destroy a village might ask: What is the justification and who is the authorizing agent for the command I am about to give? Any one of us may ask: What authorizes the change that my discourse may effect in the world? What entitles me to speak for, act for, represent the public? In the conduct of argumentation, what counts as good evidence and reasoning in the physical and social sciences, in philosophical discourse, in the courts, and in other fields? What agency, persons, or principles will authorize the terms, premises, and rules of argumentation?

We do not ordinarily require justification of things that are involuntary and natural, such as breathing, thinking, seeing. We seldom challenge even voluntary and purposeful acts: it would be odd, for example, to say that a person about to scrub the floor or work his garden should first determine that the proposed act is authorized. When we know that actions are not contrary to rule, principle, or law, or when we know that consequences are neutral or limited simply to ourselves, we usually do not request authorization.

However, authorization is needed when a proposed act or message might seriously affect the well-being of others; when an act or message, regardless of consequences, is unlawful or in some sense contrary to principle; when the agent is unable to know whether his behavior is consequential, lawful, or in agreement with principle and so needs authorization as a condition of speaking or acting in ignorance; when the agent is obliged to another person, group, or institution such that his message or action requires consent of his authorizing agency; or when a person or group claims to represent, or stand in for, another person or group.

Such conditions are familiar to anyone who has questioned whether he is properly authorized or "has the right" to speak or act. A responsible and reflective person who ventures to speak for the public—not a matter to be taken lightly—will surely pause to consider whether his discourse is accredited. Some of the above conditions apply whenever a speaker represents the public: he is standing in for it; his discourse contains premises, values, and rules of argumentation in need of authorization; and very probably his discourse affects the public's well-being. In addition, his message or its outcomes may run counter to law or principle, or he may feel compelled to speak in the absence of needed information. In many cases, the speaker will be obliged formally to the public he represents. Public speakers do actually seek to locate authoritative grounds for discourse, and we should believe that the best of them do so for the purpose of assuring that their discourse is competent and correct, and not simply for the purpose of making their discourse persuasive. Premises in the public discourse of Martin Luther King typically were truths and values authorized by divine laws, by statutes and constitutions, by principles endorsed by humane civilizations, and by the undeniable interests of a people long in bondage. Burke's speeches to the Parliament in behalf of the colonies found authoritative grounds in settled principles of English law and tradition, as well as in the aspirations of the new American public. The Declaration of Independence looked to knowledge for authorization of "self-evident truths" and to the experience of people for authorization of "facts" which documented the Crown's "repeated injuries."

In general, we may say that authorization is a power to approve, warrant, accredit, license. Throughout the centuries, it has been located variously: in the apprehension of pure reason; in mystic intuition; in the contact of mind with external reality; in the will of sovereign individuals and political entities; in the agreements of experts or of elite persons; in posterity; in the laws of God; in natural laws, processes, and rights. Whether anything at all may be authorized at some time by some ground is a question I do not now pursue. Nor do I inquire now about the nature of messages and actions which, known to lack needed authorization, risk being arbitrary, irrational, or perverse.

The central question I wish to explore is: What is the proper authorizing ground of expressions of truth and value and of judgments and actions in public rhetorical discourse? What entitles or accredits the terms, claims, and justifications of a person whose activity as speaker or audience is representative of the public? The answer to be entertained is that the public itself is the proper authorizing ground of certain terms, truths, and values justifying what is said or done in its behalf, provided that the public is competent. Further, the discourse created by a public speaker and judged by a public audience will be accredited to the extent that it competently engages or articulates the knowledge and interests of the public.

If we agree (1) that rhetorical discourse requires connection with knowledge, (2) that public rhetoric is representational, (3) that competent representation requires knowing what the public knows, and (4) that rhetoric in behalf of a public requires authorization; and if we can establish (5) that the public and it alone is the source of such knowledge that would authorize discourse and action in its behalf, and (6) that the public is competent with respect to what it may be said to know; then it will follow (7) that public rhetorical discourse must engage public knowledge.

Is the public a proper authorizing ground, and is the public competent? These questions lead us to examine John Dewey's theory of the public.

3

In 1927, John Dewey published *The Public and Its Problems*,[3] a book of extraordinary importance. Sweeping aside classical theories of politics, Dewey attempts to explain how the public and the state come into existence and how the public is to be defined. Early pages of the work distinguish between the private interaction and the public interaction. In this distinction, Dewey finds the clue to the nature and formation of publics:

> We take then our point of departure from the objective fact that human acts have consequences upon others, that some of these consequences are perceived, and that their perception leads to subsequent effort to control action so as to secure some consequences and avoid others. Following this clew, we are led to remark that the consequences are of two kinds, those which affect the persons directly engaged in a transaction, and those which affect others beyond those immediately concerned. In this distinction we find the germ of the distinction between the private and the public. When indirect consequences are recognized and there is effort to regulate them, something having the traits of a state comes into existence. When the consequences of an action are confined, or are thought to be confined, mainly to the persons directly engaged in it, the transaction is a private one (p.12).

There are, then, private acts—acts whose consequences do not extend beyond the two or three who participate; this class of acts we set aside. A second class is comprised of *public* acts: regardless of the number of persons who directly participate in action, the consequences for good or for evil extend to others—perhaps many others. This characteristic—the production of consequences affecting persons beyond ourselves—identifies a public act and creates a public. Dewey remarks, "The essence of the consequences which call a public into being is the fact that they expand beyond those directly engaged in producing them." Note that the public is *called into being* by the consequences: persons affected by such consequences comprise a public, whether or not they are aware of their identity as a public. "The public consists of all those who are affected by the indirect consequences of transactions to such an extent that it is deemed necessary to have those consequences systematically cared for." The machinery of a state—offices, officials, laws, tribunals, and the like—are invented to assure the well-being of the public.

We may say that Dewey offers a genesis theory: (1) in the first stage, public acts, as defined, occur; (2) these acts produce consequences that seriously affect the interest and well-being of persons; (3) this class of persons comprises a public; (4) the public, needing to control activities and consequences, creates offices, laws, tribunals; (5) then, says Dewey, there exists the state, which is "the organization of the public effected through officials for the protection of the interests shared by its members."

We need to clarify three points in order to appreciate Dewey's position. First, do publics come into existence and go out of existence moment by moment to the extent that there are moment by moment public transactions, each calling into existence a new and different public? Clearly, this notion is not adequate; if true, a public would have no stability. Dewey therefore qualifies the conception of consequences: the kind of consequences which carve out a public will be consequences recognized to be serious (p. 35), extensive, and enduring (p. 47) or lasting (p. 67). When transactions produce for a class of people good or evil consequences which are serious, extensive, and enduring, then that class is a public. Second, what is the relationship between a public and a state? Dewey holds that there must be a public as a condition of a state: "there is no state . . . without the public." This remark merits special notice because, as we shall observe shortly, Dewey could not easily locate the contemporary public; and if the public cannot be found, then we have cause to wonder about the nature, existence, and legitimacy of the state. A third point involves the close fit between Dewey's contextualism and his theory of the public. "In no two ages or places is there the same public," he says (p. 33). Indeed, given his views regarding the generation of publics, it must be so: transactions in Cuba will produce serious, extensive, and enduring consequences for the people of Cuba, who constitute the public there and now. But a year hence, other transactions may generate, or call into being, a different public. What is more, the public of Cuba will differ from one called into existence at the same time but in a different context, since the public is dependent on the contextual circumstances and consequences which generate it.

Dewey's view clearly permits a plurality of publics, existing simultaneously in regions, sometimes overlapping in memberships, and changing or generating anew under fresh or different circumstances in the same or in different times and places. There is, then, no public-in-the-abstract: publics are real, concrete entities comprised of people experiencing; and publics will alter in composition and nature according to the circumstances of their historic contexts.

This generative theory of the public and the state permits an easy transition to an international or universal public. In principle, the transactions of persons, or of states or publics, may produce consequences which are important, extensive, and enduring for all mankind; all human beings would then comprise a single public. We assume this universal public would include the unborn, whose fortunes are surely affected by consequences serious, enduring, and universal.

Throughout the first half of his book, Dewey writes with seeming confidence about the public and the manner of its creation. However, two major problems appear. First, looking for the contemporary United States public, Dewey cannot find it. It is, he says, in "eclipse." Where is the modern public? "If a public exists, it is surely as uncertain about its own whereabouts as philosophers since Hume have been about the residence and make-up of the self" (p. 117). Again, he asks:

> Where is the public? If there is a public, what are the obstacles in the way of its recognizing and articulating itself? Is the public a myth? Or does it come into being only in periods of marked social transition when crucial alternative issues stand out, such as that between throwing one's lot in with the conservation of established institutions or with forwarding new tendencies?

According to Dewey, the explanation of the public's eclipse and its inability to discover and articulate itself can be attributed in large part to the destruction of community by technology. The machine age has so "enormously expanded, multiplied, intensified and complicated the scope of the indirect consequences" that the public can scarcely identify itself. This is a puzzling matter. There are causes for the existence of the public, since there are consequences serious, extensive, and lasting; but the public, which in principle should be clear, sharply defined, self-aware and articulate, seems to be "not there." Why, even given the complications produced by an age of technology, should the public be in eclipse?

The second problem is hinted at in Dewey's remark about community: the technological age has caused destruction of the community. What becomes clear in the later pages of Dewey's book is that his model of the generation of a public, announced in early chapters, is incomplete: he has not specified an important condition, the existence of community. What is a community? A community is a group of persons developed through local face-to-face interactions, united in sentiment and interest, and caring for the well-being of one another. The community, he remarks, is bound together by ties "tough and subtle" and "invisible and intangible." Symbols and the communication of rich meanings are among the chief bonds of community (p. 142).

Why, then, could Dewey find no identifiable and articulate contemporary public? Because, he thought, there was no community—and because arts of communication sufficient to form community were absent. "Without such communication," he writes, "the public will remain shadowy and formless, seeking spasmodically for itself, but seizing and holding its shadow rather than its substance. Till the Great Society is converted into a Great Community, the Public will remain in eclipse. Communication can alone create a great community. Our Babel is not one of tongues but of the signs and symbols without which shared experience is impossible" (p. 142). Thus, the formation of the public requires community; and community requires the sharing of rich symbols, interests, and ideas by means of communication.

The only possible solution to our perplexity, says Dewey, is "the perfecting of the means and ways of communication of meanings so that genuinely shared interest in the consequences of interdependent activities may inform desire and effort and thereby direct action" (p. 155). A reading of Dewey suggests that the communication of which he speaks must have two objects. One object is the formation and continuity of community, and this requires the use of arts of communication for the purpose of building bonds of affection and interests among those who comprise a public; and the substance of communication will be rich uniting symbols and aspirations and a kind of wisdom which will regulate and guide the selection of long-term ends. The second object of the arts of communication will be free social inquiry, the fruits of which will enable the public to select ends and means intelligently.

I have sketched Dewey's view because all of the constituents we seek to understand have a place in his theory. The public, public knowledge or wisdom, and the arts of communication—all are present and functional. The public is called into existence in response to exigencies produced by public transactions; a growing and rich fund of knowledge, based partly in shared meanings and interests and partly in scientific inquiry, will serve the community as it moves forward through time and the circumstances of its environment; and this fund of knowledge will be subject to testing and confirmation as the public struggles with exigencies throughout its life. Rhetorical communication will enrich the public's information, sustain its experiential knowledge, and provide modes of debate and discussion needed for intelligent decision and action.

Notwithstanding the ingenuity of his position, Dewey does not satisfy on two points of special interest to us. The first has to do with the dependence of the public upon recognition of consequences of a certain kind, and the second has to do with the character of the sentiments and ideas that bond communities. First, recall that Dewey's model commences with public transactions producing serious, extensive, and enduring consequences, and that the public comes into existence as a result of its recognition that these consequences work good or evil for the persons comprising the public. How is it that persons could have the shared interests and ideas that permit them to recognize the consequences that bear upon them? Must they not comprise a community already, as a condition of their shared perceptions? I am led to believe that Dewey's model for the generation of a public requires the initial actuality of community. Moreover, apparently a community, as Dewey defines it, is essentially a public already, for it has developed shared symbols, interests, ideas, and a regard for the well-being of members. On Dewey's own principles, we would suppose that this community evolved as a result of its own activities in response to the needs and exigencies of social life. The public which Dewey saw as created by public transactions apparently already existed as a community—indeed as a public.

Second, there is a puzzle regarding the community's shared ideas, views of good and evil, interests, values—those things which bond the community and guide its choices. The presence of this fund of shared knowledge is essential not only to the conception of community but also to the evolution of a public as Dewey conceived it. But how does this knowledge come about, and how should it be characterized? I believe that the best course is to begin not with a distinction between private and public transactions and consequences, but with the actuality of publics. After we have characterized publics, we can then inquire as to what in their possession may be called public knowledge.

4

During hundreds of centuries prior to recorded history, human beings lived in communities. These communities were isolated geographically one from another and also isolated because of language, cultural, and other differences. We may assume that such communities fostered cooperative activities of work, amusement, and social intercourse to provide for the well-being of their people; toward the same end, they created organizations, offices, roles, laws, and other such instruments. A community enjoying progressive achievement through several generations could be expected to develop a fund of knowledge—knowledge that would count as principles and ends of social life, enter the day-to-day routines of physical existence, ensure the excellent performance of crafts and duties, and in some degree answer to intellectual, moral, aesthetic, and spiritual impulses. Some of this fund of knowledge would be entrusted to leaders, special offices, or groups; some would be shared by all; some would be located precariously in the records, works, and traditions of a receding past. Handed down from generation to generation, this knowledge would be improved and enlarged from time to time by means of experience, borrowing, and creative thought; due to various kinds of misfortune, parts would be lost or destroyed; and some knowledge, in the presence of altered consciousness and circumstances or put to new tests, would be abandoned or discredited.

A community, such as I have sketched, has the characteristics of a public: it consists of a class of persons sharing interests, values, meanings; it is responsive to exigencies, or problems, some of which are serious, extensive, and enduring; it seeks to attend to the well-being of its members; it has duration; it establishes numerous instruments suited to its character and needs; and it has in its possession a fund of knowledge, some part of which may be regarded as public knowledge.

Innumerable publics, differing in size and character, have existed for varying lengths of time from the beginnings of social life to the present. Most of them perished by conquest or by cultural contact and assimilation. With the death of historic publics, human achievements forever unknown to us also perished. Some publics expanded to embrace many societies and existed over centuries—for example, the massive public whose interests were protected by Roman law and institutions. Some great publics, based on other than political interests, crossed national boundaries: Christianity and other world religions embraced huge publics whose most vital interests were thought to be guided by religious knowledge and institutions. In modern times, a very influential transcultural public, neither political nor religious, is the scientific community—the class of persons of scientific temperament and commitment. This community seems increasingly uncomfortable, for it lacks contact with truths and values beyond the reach of its methods—humane wisdom that could give it competence to deal with the most vivid problems facing mankind. Contemporary political publics exist in large numbers and range from semiprimitive tribes, which are largely isolated from other peoples, to the more or less cohesive publics associated with sovereign nations. And within nations, such as the United States, there are subordinate publics, political and otherwise, some of which struggle to maintain their identity in the face of strong pressure toward disintegration.

Is it possible to uncover public knowledge by recording everything that the members of a public profess to know explicitly, on the assumption that all propositions believed and expressed will count as public knowledge? This would not take us in the direction we seek. First, such a procedure would uncover all sorts of propositions—that water quenches thirst, that all persons deserve to be free, that some plants are edible and others are not, that two is half of four, that the book is on the desk—a miscellany of facts, rules, principles, conventions, laws, and the like, some of which are authorized by agencies other than the public and some of which are false. Second, such an approach assumes that the public knowledge is expressed in the language of the public and thus could be uncovered by examining its utterances—a dangerous assumption; it is conceivable that some important public knowledge is not propositional and not expressed in language. Finally, public knowledge might be in the possession of a very small fraction of the persons comprising a public; if we ask what is known by nearly all members of a public, we might miss the most important constituents. We must conclude, then, that public knowledge is not identical with everything the public believes and can express: the public undoubtedly knows and believes more than its public knowledge; some part of its public knowledge may be nonpropositional; and some public knowledge may be known to only a few.

Public knowledge, it may be suggested, can be regarded as that set of truths and values which would characterize a competent public. Any physician, if he is to be judged competent, ought to possess a certain body of knowledge. Thus, we might assert that there is a body of public knowledge that any public, to be judged competent, must possess. There are serious drawbacks, however, to this line of thought. First, it is doubtful that we can know what knowledge would be needed by a physician a hundred or thousand years hence; neither can we foresee just what knowledge ought to characterize a future public. Secondly, the present knowledge needed by a physician in one context may differ strikingly from that needed by another in a very different context; in like manner, the knowledge which now would make Public A competent may not necessarily make Public B competent. The most serious drawback, however, is the assumption that there can be a public knowledge *a priori*. This assumption must be dismissed because it runs counter to consideration of whether the public itself authorizes public knowledge.

Public knowledge, at its most fundamental level, must be distinguished from private knowledge and from private knowledge made general. Public knowledge is located and can only be located in the public, and is authorized and can only be authorized by the public. Private knowledge, on the other hand, consists of truths that can be known to individuals by means of observation and inquiry: for example, fire against one's skin produces pain, the sun sets in the west, or a particular combination of metals makes a good cooking pot. Private knowledge made general refers to private truths that may be shared widely or even transmitted from one generation to another, but which are capable in principle of being discovered anew by individuals and authorized by some ground other than the public. Public knowledge may be known to individuals and very often is sustained or carried by a public, but it differs strikingly from private knowledge and from private knowledge made general: the truths of public knowledge, lacking a public, have no status, no authorization, indeed no existence.

A clue to the nature of public knowledge is to be found in the distinction between truths which exist independent of human participation and truths which owe their existence to human participation. This distinction may be easily admitted, for we are aware that bare facts differ from facts which, when related to our interests, become weighted facts or items of personal knowledge—that is, facts or truths whose existence requires our personal subjectivity. Dewey expresses the distinction by noting that "the difference between facts which are what they are independent of human desire and endeavor and facts which are to some extent what they are because of human interest and purpose, and which alter with alteration in the latter, cannot be got rid of by any methodology" (p. 7). Similarly, Michael Polanyi holds that "to the extent to which our personal participation in knowing a fact contributes to making it what it is, we may call it a *personal fact.*"[4] There are in the physical world literally billions of factual conditions—bare facts—which, when known to us, do not engage our interested participation in such ways that our participation weights or transforms them. Thus, in an ordinary case, what we may discover as facts about the planet Mars are bare facts; our interest in those facts, curiosity perhaps, will not transform them. In the physical universe there are facts, organizations of facts, and laws of nature awaiting discovery and expression. Aspiration to discover and express such facts and laws may motivate search, but the facts and laws of the physical universe are what they are irrespective of our aspiration. On the other hand, the experiential world presents to us many weighted or personal facts which are what they are because our participation gives them a status and invests them with a value they would not otherwise enjoy. As our participation varies, the personal facts vary; and in the absence of our participation, the personal facts cease to exist. What elements of human subjectivity have this transforming power? The answer appears to be: our interests, principles, values, definitions, maxims, conceptual systems. These rather stable elements of our mental life transform things and events into personal facts. These transforming elements, I shall assume, exist in human subjectivity and nowhere else. Thus the remote and disinterested observer of a child wasting from disease observes a purely factual condition, while the mother whose love embraces the child witnesses real tragedy. The mother's love, existing in her and nowhere else, is precisely the condition or element which transforms bare facts into personal facts; the personal facts would not exist in the absence of her loving participation.

Because our subjectivity enters into and sustains personal facts, it might be said that individuals are the ground and authority of all the personal facts in our experience. To an extent this is true, but in a very important respect we individuals are not the sole ground and authority of our personal facts, because the constituents of personal facts are not made by us. We stand in a double relation—to the world of facts and to the realm of our mental life; both of these constituents, mediated by the individual in experience, contribute to the creation of personal facts. The world of facts—the world as it is—is not created by the individual; nor can a significant part of the stable elements of mental life—interests, definitions, values, maxims, and the like—be created by an individual in the span of a lifetime. Both the world of facts and the realm of mental life, to the extent that they enter our experience, serve as grounds or authority for our personal facts. The individual is delicately positioned between facts, given by the world as it is, and the elements of mental life, most of which he inherits from the publics in which he dwells.

The public, as a collective body or community of persons sharing inherited elements of mental life, gives existence to personal or subjective facts in the same way as the individual. Purely factual conditions experienced by the public come into relation with shared sentiments, principles, and values that characterize persons not as individuals but as members of the public; and the power of participation transforms those factual conditions into the public's personal facts. Such facts will exist as long as the public's experience sustains them. The public which witnessed with sorrow and lamentation the death of Martin Luther King, Jr., will continue to sustain that tragic personal fact as long as the memory is vivid and the sentiments are constant. The public's personal facts owe their existence to the shared subjective experience; in the absence of this experience the public would have no personal facts. In this sense, the public is the ground and the authority of all of its personal facts, which count therefore as part of public knowledge. A widespread recognition of personal facts serves as a sign of the existence of a public, and the number and variety of commonly acknowledged personal facts will be indicative of the public's homogeneity and of its breadth of concern.

Both the influence and source of the elements of mental life deserve our notice. The influence is clearly powerful—so powerful that a purely factual condition may be transformed into contrary personal facts because of the power of contrary interests, values, and perspectives. Even without a direct relation to the world of fact, elements of mental life powerfully influence one another: for example, a person may judge in the conduct of dialectic that some definitions or principles which he embraces must be abandoned or altered because they do not agree with other definitions or principles that have greater force. The source of the elements of mental life is complex. First, it is oneself; individual subjectivity seems to be the original ground of passions and of some interests, and mental elements would have no influence except through the individual's own mediation. Second, the source is clearly other than the individual; the individual creates or discovers not more than a fragment of such stable elements as definitions, values, principles, and conceptual systems. If there is a public knowledge in addition to the personal facts created by a public, then the constituents of this knowledge would seem to reside in the elements of mental life which publics create or sustain, and which so powerfully influence the personal facts of our individual and collective experience.

The Declaration of Independence may be viewed as a clear instance of discourse utilizing and expressing public knowledge. We note first the statements in the second paragraph:

> We hold these truths to be self-evident, that all men are created equal, that they are endowed by their Creator with certain unalienable Rights, that among these are Life, Liberty, and the Pursuit of Happiness. That to secure these rights, Governments are instituted among Men, deriving their just powers from the consent of the governed. That whenever any Form of Government becomes destructive of these ends, it is the Right of the People to alter or to abolish it, and to institute new Government, laying its foundation on such principles and organizing its powers in such form, as to them shall seem most likely to effect their Safety and Happiness. Prudence, indeed, will dictate that Governments long established should not be changed for light and transient causes; and accordingly all experience hath shown, that mankind are more disposed to suffer, while evils are sufferable, than to right themselves by abolishing the forms to which they are accustomed. But when a long train of abuses and usurpations, pursuing invariably the same Object, evinces a design to reduce them under absolute Despotism, it is their right, it is their duty, to throw off such Government, and to provide new Guards for their future security. . . .

In overall design, the Declaration is a rhetorical deductive argument—an enthymeme or set of enthymemes—consisting of major premises contained in the second paragraph and minor premises supported by the listing of many particular instances of the Crown's "repeated injuries."

We need not examine in detail the statements in that second paragraph: the affirmations of values, principles, maxims of political life, and probabilities—all calculated to be sufficient to win the assent of a "candid world"—are surely recognizable. Note that they are affirmed as unassailable truths; their claim upon our apprehension is regarded as so decisive and powerful that they merit the strong form of commitment, self-evidence. Are these axioms—these self-evident truths—the product of scientific investigation? Clearly not. Are they self-evident in the sense that they could not be denied without producing contradiction? They can be denied. They are not authorized by scientific inquiry; they are not tautologies. What then authorizes them? They are authorized by a community with a history and tradition in which these truths grew and were accredited. These principles and truths, rooted in the past, framed the aspirations and objectives of the American revolutionaries, and they continue to serve as principles of public life—constituents of public knowledge.

Consider for a moment the abuses cited in the Declaration. The long list comprises the body of the document, but three examples will suffice. What are the "repeated injuries" of which the colonists complain? The Crown

> . . . has kept among us, in times of peace, Standing Armies without the Consent of our legislatures.
>
> He has dissolved Representative Houses repeatedly, for opposing with manly firmness his invasions on the rights of the people.
>
> He has plundered our seas, ravaged our Coasts, burnt our towns, and destroyed the lives of our people.

Now, these are not bare facts, though they might count as such to an observer remote and indifferent. These factual conditions, when related to felt interests and principles, become transformed: they become grievances, injuries, injustices—precisely because the factual conditions stand in relation to interests and passions and to laws, rights, and principles which this public affirms. They count as decisive personal facts.

What, then, shall we understand public knowledge to consist of? I do not pretend to make an exhaustive list, but the constituents surely include: principles of public life to which we submit as conditions of living together; shared interests and aspirations; values which embody our common goals and virtues; our constitutions, laws, and rules; definitions and conceptual systems; truths expressed in literatures of poetry, criticism, philosophy, aesthetics, politics, and science; the accumulated wisdom proffered by our cultural pasts; and, to these, we add the personal facts of our public life. This conception of public knowledge very nearly coincides with what Michael Polanyi names "superior knowledge." He writes: "I shall regard the entire culture of a modern, highly articulate community as a form of superior knowledge. This superior knowledge will be taken to include, therefore, beside the systems of science and other factual truths, all that is coherently believed to be right and excellent by men within their culture." Where does this knowledge reside? "Only a small fragment of his own culture is directly visible to any of its adherents. Large parts of it are altogether buried in books, paintings, musical scores, etc., which remain mostly unread, unseen, unperformed. The messages of these records live, even in the minds best informed about them, only in their awareness of having access to them and of being able to evoke their voices and understand them."[5] This conception of public knowledge includes also what Walter Lippmann understood to be kinds of truths needed in a "public philosophy." The truths, he writes, "are the laws of a rational order of human society—in the sense that all men, when they are sincerely and lucidly rational, will regard them as self-evident. The rational order consists of the terms which must be met in order to fulfill men's capacity for the good life in this world. They are the terms of the widest consensus of rational men in a plural society. They are the propositions to which all men concerned, if they are sincerely and lucidly rational, can be expected to converge."[6]

A public possesses what I have called public knowledge both among the constituents of its mental life, such as those we have noted, and among its personal facts. In the absence of this knowledge, there is no genuine public, but only an artificial one consisting of a population held together by such forces as coercive regulations and unchangeable boundaries. A public is identifiable as such to the extent that it articulates significant parts of its knowledge and experiences personal facts in its public life. The public that would maintain its identity will learn, rehearse, and celebrate what it knows; it will not only experience its personal facts, but also will display and sometimes dramatize them. If a public loses acquaintance with its inherited knowledge, it will at the same time lose common recognition of personal facts, because it cannot experience personal facts unless its inherited knowledge enters its experience. A public that is progressively impoverished by decreasing contact with its inherited knowledge and by a concommitant incapacity to experience shared personal facts is moving toward disintegration and loss of identity. A public "in eclipse" actually may be an artificial public, a public lacking able spokesmen, a public split into fragments which may or may not develop into articulate publics, or a public moving toward disintegration.

The public serves as the authorizing ground or agent of its public knowledge. First, the personal facts, which comprise one part, are what they are because of the public's subjective experience. No person or group, whether related or not to the public's mental life, could authorize or accredit a personal fact for the public, though anyone might submit experiences to the public to be accredited by it. If the public's personal facts are created because of the transforming power of elements of the public's mental life and if the public's mental life is authorized only by the public, then no agency other than the public can authorize its personal facts. Second, the public's constituents of mental life—interests, values, principles, etc.— which provide the location of the remainder of its public knowledge, not only reside in the public's consciousness or in its tradition, but have no status as truths or principles except that which is provided by the public's power of authorization. A person, group, or a document from the past may present a new principle or value of potential worth, but that principle or value will become authoritative only when submitted to the public and accepted by it. Of what does this power of authorization consist? It consists, first, of the recognition by the public of the essential truth, rightness, or fitness of its personal facts and of the items of its inherited knowledge; and second, of the continued affirmation of that knowledge which merits continued affirmation because it contributes to the public's achievements.

I do not mean to imply that the knowledge characterizing a public will be unchanging, known to all, fully explicit, and infallible. Public knowledge will change as new conceptions, values, and principles are added and old ones discarded, and as some of these recede into the background while others become dominant. The whole fund of public knowledge will not be known to all living adult members of a public. However, certain salient elements will be known to most—if those elements are placed regularly before the public view. Some will be known well by a few members and by institutions and organizations charged with knowing and sustaining them. What is more, members will know salient elements in varying degrees: although nearly all members may celebrate a principle, only a few persons may fully understand and appreciate it. Much of the public knowledge will be explicit in the sense that it can be stated and affirmed. But some will be below the surface of public consciousness, awaiting announcement. A level of public knowledge may also exist that is essentially inarticulate, such as one's awareness of community and of those bonds of friendship and affection held by Dewey to be "invisible and intangible." Finally, we observe that some parts of public knowledge will be matters in contention to be decided one way or the other, or perhaps never winning full endorsement but never quite repudiated; some professed truths will be false, some mere opinion. This reflects the fact that a public, no less than an individual, is subject to error and correction and that it sustains kinds of knowledge that do not easily win recognition as truths.

Public knowledge may be tested through numerous means. First, insofar as the personal facts in the experience of a public refer to objective factual conditions, empirical observation and testing will be appropriate in order to determine whether the facts entering experience are indeed what we believe them to be. Second, if the objective component of a personal fact is correct, then the personal fact may be dramatized, analyzed, or placed in juxtaposition to competing personal facts in order to recognize its qualities and implications. This task is often performed by works of poetry and criticism. Third, the items of inherited knowledge, insofar as they comprise systems that exhibit coherence within and among themselves as well as integration with our personal facts, may be examined and corrected dialectically by persons who understand them and appreciate their force. Fourth, the testing of public knowledge also occurs in the successive and overlapping rhetorical situations which the public encounters as it interacts with its total environment. In its dramatic life, the public is presented with problems or exigencies, large and small, which must be modified positively in order to assure existence and achievement. Public spokesmen create discourse that expresses and generates public knowledge; they debate, judge, celebrate, and make appeal to the community of feeling and ideas. Principles, values, and truths thought to be already accredited may be discredited and either abandoned or revised in the course of struggle; and a public, in attempting to modify exigencies, may posit new values and truths which win approval because they are perceived to be manifestly right or fit.

Competence is skillful employment of knowledge in performing tasks, in making things for use or enjoyment, in judging things according to their truth, justness, propriety, and beauty, and in ordering things toward desired outcomes. A competent public is one that is well equipped with public knowledge. A public with broad concerns, with a rich fund of knowledge, and with skillful speakers and audiences will be competent. Insofar as a public enriches its fund of public knowledge, it becomes increasingly competent and in command of authority; as a public suffers loss of public knowledge, its competence and its authority are diminished. In the absence of public knowledge, there is no competence, no authorization, and no public.

Wordsworth's lines in "Observations" provide an apt statement of the relation among competence, knowledge, and authorization:

Aristotle, I have been told, has said, that Poetry is the most philosophical of all writing: it is so: its object is truth, not individual and local, but general, and operative; not standing upon external testimony, but carried alive into the heart by passion; truth which is its own testimony, which gives competence and confidence to the tribunal to which it appeals, and receives them from the same tribunal.

In relation to our topic, Wordsworth's thought comes to this: the poets, the orators, the prophets, the men and women of vision—all those who in some way give expression to truth and submit their discovery or invention to the tribunal, which is the public, do thereby give competence and confidence to the public; and the public confirms the truths offered to it, and is thus enriched.

5

The exigencies of our time are dangerous almost beyond the power of imagination to conceive: war, famine, threat of accidental destruction by instruments of technology, ruin of an irreplaceable environment—these and other exigencies threaten to destroy individuals and societies. The exigencies are global, and no less than a universal public is sufficient to authorize their modification. Prudence bids us set a course toward global civilization and creation of a public embracing all mankind. Surely we seek conditions in which modification of dangerous global exigencies is feasible, in which divisive competitions give way to cooperative growth, in which human beings find satisfactions of physical wants and, moreover, enjoy an intellectual and aesthetic life marked by ease of spirit and achievement in knowing and doing. These ends require an art of life. An art of life requires a wisdom—both knowledge and method.

Rhetoric's task in this new and dangerous age is to assist the formulation and creation of that knowledge and method constitutive of wisdom characterizing a universal public. This universal public will serve as the authoritative agency of decision and action needed to reduce contemporary anxieties and to provide conditions of universal culture. The central goal of rhetorical practice, therefore, is the Isocratic goal—to fashion means and provide impetus toward civilization, with regard to all humanity. An art of discourse—a knowledge and method—sufficient to this achievement is the practical rhetoric we seek.

The principal goal of rhetorical theory and criticism is to assist the invention of discourse—both content and form, both methods of creation and acts of presentation—by which rhetorical practice may succeed in giving substance and voice to the universal public. One element of this task is the recovery of old and the formulation of new public knowledge sufficient to the needs of the age and its problems.

Rich funds of public knowledge in our cultural pasts must be redis-covered; the public knowledge that now exists just below the surface of our awareness must be announced by persons of insight and eloquence; and the knowledge which would characterize a universal public must be organized and created by those capable of seeing and voicing the conditions and interests, the values and truths of a public capable of overcoming hazards to be encountered. It is not inevitable that contemporary spokesmen and publics will tap the best of public knowledge: there is danger that the best will remain unavailable to them.

Man alone, so far as we know, has the capacity to find and create truths which can serve as constituents of the art of life. But there are obstacles and tendencies which thwart generation and recognition of this knowledge. The first is limited individual existence. As indi-viduals we are granted but a short and precious span of existence, hardly enough to acquire the wisdom we need. We can borrow from our contemporaries, but they, like ourselves, suffer the limited vision of brief experience. The second is the countervailing forces of false opinion, poverty of sentiment, and bleak physical conditions. The third is our tendency to yield to the claims of present circum-stances, needs, and desires which, while valid in themselves, dis-tract us from enduring truths and separate us from the wisdom of tradition. The fourth is our habit of regarding as true—as knowledge—those propositions which issue from accepted scien-tific procedures of investigation and confirmation. As a result, prin-ciples of moral conduct and maxims of political and social life—indeed all of humane wisdom that may guide civilization—have been regarded as opinion found wanting when put to the tests of confirmation. A fifth and related cause is the widespread current belief that truth is to be found in *this* slice of time—in the here and now, in this set of experiences, during this present inquiry, this year. We seem unable or unwilling to acknowledge that some truths are not to be found in these kinds of time frames, but rather *become*, over time, and perhaps pass in and out of existence. Why should we not acknowledge that some truths exist as faint rays of light, per-ceived perhaps dimly in a near-forgotten past, but which light up again and again in the experience of generations? Finally, our gen-eral suspicion of tradition cuts us off from a rich fund of knowledge. We lose important wisdom which ought to be brought into the present where it may enrich culture and assist the resolution of problems.

The great task of rhetorical theory and criticism, then, is to un-cover and make available the public knowledge needed in our time and to give body and voice to the universal public. In the absence of a developing universal public and of knowledge and method sufficient to the problems of the time, our hopes for the future surely will be dulled by almost inevitable alternatives: either regimentation and coercion of persons and publics that have been heretofore relatively free and self-determining, or steady deterioration of the conditions of life.

Literature
and Politics

Donald C. Bryant

I am indeed pleased to have a part in this interdisciplinary seminar. Things interdisciplinary of late have become newly fashionable; but I have never been anything but interdisciplinary in my teaching and scholarship. In pursuit of rhetoric and public address I have always moved freely—sometimes, no doubt, recklessly—through literature, history, drama, and criticism. At no time, though, have I presumed to pass as philosopher.

My function in your learned galaxy I assume to be not innovation but confirmation or restoration. Lloyd Bitzer brings something new and innovative. Kenneth Burke adds fresh insights into what he has said and written in the past. I, however, have nothing brand new to advance, nor interesting amendments to my earlier pronouncements; but in restoration I can feel more or less comfortable—not in conjuring up anachronistic specters of a departed past, but rather in the honorable venture of brushing archival dust from certain old concepts and truths which have flourished and ought to flourish again.

In bringing together once again rhetoric, literature, and philosophy, it seems to me that you revive the possibility of a new Ciceronian union of wisdom and eloquence. The more we seek to unite rhetoric, literature, and philosophy in common belletristic ventures, the nearer we bring rebirth of, shall we say, the seventeenth-century Frenchman Rapin's concept of *L'Éloquence*, arising from the interaction of these three studies plus history. I do not for a moment suggest abandoning or denigrating that study of rhetoric which attends to social movements and what Bitzer calls "public knowledge"—which, for example, explains black rhetoric, "plumbers'" rhetoric, or the sloganeering of public relations and election campaigns. The scope and emphasis of this seminar, however, permit us to examine less ordinary concerns and concepts also.

Hence I venture upon "Literature and Politics."

Perhaps that is a pretentious title for a lecture by a professor of speech—a rhetorician; but as I have reminded my readers in a recent essay,[1] Herbert Wichelns in his often misread essay on "The Literary Criticism of Oratory" found rhetorical criticism lying "at the boundary of politics (in the broadest sense) and literature." He found its atmosphere "that of public life" and its concern "with the ideas of people as influenced by their leaders."[2] Those concepts I certainly share, and I propose to elaborate upon them.

Now if I were a Winston Churchill, I think no one would find me presumptuous or pretentious undertaking a discourse on literature and politics. Sir Winston, we are willing to confess, was great in politics—at least the grand politics of war—and he spoke literature almost by nature (as I have said on other occasions[3]) whenever charged circumstances generated in him that magnitude of thought, that splendor of language, the power of those images, the dynamic movement of the rhythm of delivery with which we are familiar—some of us from the naked ear, others from print and sound recordings:

> Never in the field of human conflict was so much owed by so many to so few.

> We shall fight on the beaches, we shall fight on the landing grounds, we shall fight in the fields and in the streets, we shall fight in the hills; we shall never surrender.

That is the Churchill we are familiar with and many of us admire. How far is it from the Blake who wrote,

> I will not cease from mental fight,
> Nor shall my sword sleep in my hand
> Till we have built Jerusalem
> In England's green and pleasant land? *(Milton)*

Even on occasions something short of grand, however—though in a measure splendid nevertheless—the touch of literature seemed to descend upon a Churchillian idea. I heard him, for example, in 1951 when he was making a ceremonial visit to the then black and drizzling steel center of Sheffield in Yorkshire[4]—a 60 percent Socialist city receiving in triumph the war-time leader of England, who was then only the head of the Tory party out of power. But Sheffield is not only the soundest and soberest of the Labour towns. It is the center of the heavy steel industry and the home of fine cutlery and of the famous "Sheffield plate."

The manufacturers of this steel and this cutlery have for centuries associated themselves in the Master Cutlers' Society. Once a year the wealth of the industry assembles for its glory and its profit at the Master Cutlers' Feast in an atmosphere and an environment of luxury, of conspicuous and traditional extravagance, to drink, to dine, to display its magnificence and its women, and to hear an address on matters of weight and moment. Perhaps things are different now, but twenty-odd years ago the women sat not at the banqueting tables but in a balcony, visible but apart.

In the spring of 1951, like this spring [1974], a Labour government occupied the offices in Whitehall. It proceeded apace with the nationalization of basic industries. The magnates of the Master Cutlers' Society, however, were still actually free. Though nominally nationalized, as yet steel in fact throve under private management. At any time, however, the government might feel strong enough and well enough equipped to move in and take over. When the greatest of the Tories, therefore, should visit the municipal corporation of Sheffield, what more proper than that he should come at the time of the great Conservative event, that he should speak to the populace of the Socialist city one evening after a triumphal procession through the streets, and that he should address the master cutlers the next? He did.

I do not propose to review those speeches. At best they were topical and for Churchill more or less routine. They were made to fit occasions short of grand—though in a measure splendid nonetheless—and Churchill filled the occasions without inflating them. From the master cutlers' speech I remember the central figure (which I have since verified from the press), which tempted me into this account. It is the image of the Steel Corporation (that is the Socialist) vulture, with its two grasping claws, Uniformity and Monopoly, drifting and circling above the furnaces and yards of Sheffield steel. That image synthesized at once—it did not merely decorate—the situation of the industry as Churchill saw it and wanted his audience to see it; and I think that is the kind of function we expect of images in poetry, that is, in literature. The full meaning and special force of the image, of course, were complete only in the atmosphere and circumstances of its birth in a characteristically Churchillian parturition. Constructed slowly, grimly, and ponderously, as the carrion birds themselves do float above their potential prey, the image became the incarnation of portentous reality. The bird, Sir Winston concluded, would finally drop—exhausted and unfed!

Out of context and recounted here by me, the image is no doubt laughable. In its natal circumstances it was not. As I wrote in an earlier essay, using an expression of Northrop Frye's:

Characteristic of this discourse is a live articulation of meaning. . . . It is

Donald C. Bryant

genuine *fusion* of thought, feelings, and expression, not simply the
manipulation of thought, feeling, and expression. I am suggesting,
therefore, that a radical quality of the best of [public] political discourse
is this articulation of emotion, this metaphor. I suggest also that one of
the functions of literature, sometimes at least, may be imaginatively to
organize idea and emotion . . . toward political enlightenment or action,
and not merely or solely to articulate idea and emotion [as experience].
Here literature and politics join on their common ground, the
rhetorical.[5]

The highest elevations of that common ground exhibit what we
know as eloquence.

But I am no Churchill, and you will require of me further justification for coupling literature and politics. Nor am I a special student of
Sir Winston and his eloquence. Perhaps another illustration not
unrelated to the last and closer to my own special study may help us
approach the essence of what I am talking about. Let me turn to
another well-known writer and speaker—man of letters—thriving
in the contexts of politics and literature, who often gave to his
discourse upon the problems of social philosophy and political
action the stature of literature. Of course I mean Burke—Edmund,
that is, Burke *minor* in this seminar—the friend of Dr. Johnson, Sir
Joshua Reynolds, Oliver Goldsmith, the American colonies, the
British constitution, the Sublime and Beautiful, and even, until
1790, of Tom Paine.

I do not accept the position of some of Burke's friends, such as
Goldsmith, that he should never have given up literature for politics. I do defend, however, the notion that Burke spoke and wrote
literature in the immediate and the ultimate contexts in which he
operated—not always, and often not brilliantly, but often enough,
and superbly when subject and occasion conspired with full mind,
strong feeling, and articulate purpose. Of course, what used to get
into the old sophomore anthologies of English literature (when
there was still a market for them) was not necessarily literature by
your standards; and what constitutes required reading, if any, in
English classes in high school becomes less and less literary as social
adaptation submerges intellectual, imaginative, and emotional
maturity in the supposed needs of the functioning citizen. Even so
late as my high school years, however, Burke's *Speech on Conciliation
with America* was standard reading for the fourth year (not in social
studies or in an integrated program but in English), along with
Macbeth, The Canterbury Tales, and *Comus.* That classic discourse had
not yet been elevated to the second year of graduate study in the
department of speech. Burke's declamation beginning "The proposition is peace. Not peace through the medium of war; not peace to
be hunted through the labyrinth of intricate and endless negotia-

tions; not peace to rise out of universal discord, fomented from principle," and his famous "character" of the Americans in that speech exhibit qualities usually attributed to prose literature, and most of the characteristics of poetry—except a technical detachment from "the world of social action and event." Let us taste that second passage though out of its context. Burke is breathing articulate life (for the House of Commons and later for his readers) into the statistics on colonial commerce which are before the Commons for all to ignore.

> As to the wealth which the colonies have drawn from the sea by their fisheries. . . , pray, Sir, what in the world is equal to it? Pass by the other parts, and look at the manner in which the people of New England have of late carried on the whale-fishery. Whilst we follow them among the tumbling mountains of ice, and behold them penetrating into the deepest frozen recesses of Hudson's Bay and Davis's Straits, whilst we are looking for them beneath the arctic circle, we hear that they have pierced into the opposite region of polar cold, that they are at the antipodes, and engaged under the frozen serpent of the south. . . . We know that whilst some of them draw the line and strike the harpoon on the coast of Africa, others run the longitude and pursue their gigantic game along the coast of Brazil. No sea but what is vexed by their fisheries [and so on].[6]

That is not Melville hunting Moby Dick, to be sure, but it is close to Richard Henry Dana's *Two Years Before the Mast;* and had Robinson Crusoe tracked the leviathan, Defoe would have been taxed to equal that passage from Burke. That is not an "hypothetical verbal structure which exists for its own sake."[7] It is imaginative creation in the service of rhetorical purpose. It is literature and politics, or better literature-politics acting as one. Whether in such passages as I have just quoted or in the nowadays better-known *Reflections on the Revolution in France* with its oft-cited apostrophe to the queen of France and its pictures of the capture and humiliation of Louis and Marie-Antoinette; or in Burke's last great work, the apologia-repartee *Letter to a Noble Lord,* with its deadly contrast of Burke and the young Duke of Bedford, with its noble portrait of the triple keep of Windsor, the symbol of the British Constitution, with its equal and coeval towers—there "the imagination informs the politics and energizes it; the metaphor (as Hazlitt and others have suggested) does not [merely] decorate the thought, it incarnates the thought, it creates the idea. That is the realm of Longinus."[8]

Burke brought literature to politics, to be sure. His education, his occupation before he came to public affairs and after, was literary in the broadest sense—a sense which our current distinction between humanities and social sciences may tend to obscure. But not only did he bring a literary domestication to politics; he functioned in what seems to me a characteristically literary way in his rhetorical-political writing and speaking. The evidence of his habits of composing shows that to Burke thinking, imagining, writing, and speaking became together one single, unified activity or experience, creating of politics, at its best, literature, at least as Lord Morley thought of it when he wrote, "Literature consists of all the books—and they are not so many—where moral truth and human passion are touched with a certain largeness, sanity, and attraction of form."[9] I have found it illuminating to think of Burke's output in three successive stages: **literature** and politics, **politics** and literature, and finally the **literature** of **politics**.

Now if you interdisciplinary humanists *cum* crossbred social scientists will allow me a conception of literature which will include the best of Burke and Churchill—Morley's conception perhaps, or any other which embodies the idea of imaginative creation of human social value in the medium of language—we might agree that in the Anglo-Irishman and the descendant of Marlborough the union of literature and politics reached two of its highest crests in modern times. We might then stand upon the traditional ground that eloquence is one of the principal modes of literature and that it is at the same time one of the principal dynamics of politics. Perhaps then we might extend eloquence in this dual role beyond "speeches," "oratory" oral and written, to those compositions of the polemicists, the publicists, the teachers and leaders of men which are "touched with a certain largeness, sanity, and attractiveness of form"; and also to those works of the poets and men of letters which grapple more or less directly with life and society in heaven and earth—to Swift's *Drapier* and his *Gulliver*, to Milton in much of *Samson Agonistes* and *Paradise Lost*, to Bunyan's *Pilgrim's Progress*, Whitman's *Leaves of Grass*, and Steinbeck's *Grapes of Wrath*. Perhaps we might then agree that it is critically and conceptually profitable to think that as Burke spoke and wrote literature, so did Shakespeare, Milton, Dickens, and Shaw, for example, often illumine politics in a large and legitimate sense.

I present these considerations concerning literature and politics as representing *contested* positions because I think in fact that in academic circles and among certain numerous literary critics as well as social scientists they are contested *theoretically* if not always actually in practice. Perhaps in the last few years, in the new surge of literature-with-thesis as academic offering—black literature, Afro-American literature, Chicano literature, women's literature, with their frank and patent rhetorical biases—we are tending operationally to accept public social-political functions for "literature," but not yet, I think, do we accept them with comfort theoretically. Long plagued with the recurrent suspicion that they were not teaching literature at all but a low-grade sort of social history and gossipy biography, professors of literature strove mightily to shuck off their load of extraneous matter. And truly they were fairly successful in getting rid of much of the biography, most of the history, large blocks of the sociology, the economics, the politics, and the psychology. In this campaign they were certainly encouraged by many varieties of new critics all having in common at least an explicit or tacit resolve as critics to do otherwise than Matthew Arnold whenever possible.

As a reaction against an excessive tendency to study literature primarily as a magazine of interesting materials for cultural history, philosophy, or behavioral science, the search for the characteristically literary way to study literature has yielded many admirable results. We couldn't have done without our Allen Tates, our Empsons, our Welleks, our Brooks and Warrens, our Murry Kriegers, to mention only a few. On the other hand, the proposition that the *whole* duty of the professor of literature or of the literary critic is to examine the "poem *qua* poem," that is, as a hypothetical construction of language, whose atom is the metaphor, existing for its own sake—this proposition, *I* find, leaves something important still to be desired in the study of literature. At least it shifts some of the main burden onto others who have no traditional claim to literature as their material and little academic stake in literature as the verbal expression of the most significant qualities of man in civilized society.

One of the brightest of my former colleagues once maintained with becoming vehemence that the only business of the critic is to "show how the poem is made." For *poem* read, of course, *novel, play, story, film,* what you will. Though this goal as he interpreted it permitted *him* to bring anything he chose to bear upon the study of literature, the statement was the sort of thing which underlies that literary study which attends wholly to the consideration of internal form. The late Bernard Weinberg was probably one of the wisest and best examples of that basis of analysis.

Now I understand the position and I would not try to overturn it—completely. It *must* be one of the positions taken toward literary study (at least for healthily polemical purposes) to keep us all from becoming bad sociologists and pseudo political scientists. I would wish only to modify the sense of functional isolation which it creates around literature.

It ought to be evident, for better or for worse, that in speaking of literature and politics I favor a view in which politics comprehends broadly the movement of power in the state—or the world—and a view, further, in which literature has what Plato required of it, what Sir Philip Sidney prized as one of its glories, what other literary theorists have historically claimed for it—a social-rhetorical mission rightly and characteristically its own. This view has never entirely disappeared from currency, but there are times, and the present and recent past are among them, when it is hard, it appears, to sail under the colors of *literary* scholar and critic and endorse, for example, the underlying proposition of a cultural commentator like Lionel Trilling.

In the preface to his collection of essays called *The Liberal Imagination*, Professor Trilling quotes Charles Péguy's aphorism "Tout commence en mystique et finit en politique," which he then paraphrases as "everything begins in sentiment and assumption and finds its issue in political action and institutions." The converse, Trilling goes on, is also true: "Just as sentiments become ideas, ideas eventually establish themselves as sentiments." I take that to mean that the conscious idea becomes quieted into the uncontested ground for political response. Let us follow Trilling further:

> If this is so, if between sentiments and ideas there is a natural connection so close as to amount to a kind of identity, then the connection between literature and politics will be seen as a very immediate one. And this will seem especially true if we do not intend the narrow but the wide sense of the word politics. It is the wide sense of the word that is nowadays forced upon us, for clearly it is no longer possible to think of politics except as the politics of culture, the organization of human life toward some end or other, toward the modification of sentiments, which is to say the quality of human life. . . . [The essays in this book] are not political essays, they are essays in literary criticism. But they assume the inevitable intimate, if not always obvious, connection between literature and politics.
>
> The making of the connection requires . . . no great ingenuity, nor any extravagant manipulation of the word literature or, beyond taking it in the large sense specified, of the word politics. It is a connection which is quickly understood and as quickly acted upon by certain governments. And although it is often resisted by many very good literary critics, it has for some time been accepted with enthusiasm by the most interesting of our creative writers; the literature of the modern period, of the last century and a half, has been characteristically political. Of the writers of the last hundred and fifty years who command our continuing attention, the very large majority have in one way or another turned their passions, their adverse, critical, and very intense passions, upon the condition of the polity.[10]

Shall I settle for this passage from Trilling as a sufficient summary of my principal proposition so far? I think I shall add, with your permission, a sentence or so from the fifth part of *Educating Liberally* by Hoyt H. Hudson, a splendid little book which might well be the principal text, or at least the initial text, for our interdisciplinary preoccupation with education in a computerized future. Hudson was one of the early Cornell rhetorical scholars, an editor of the *Quarterly Journal of Speech* in the early 1930s, who became a distinguished scholar in Renaissance English literature at Princeton and Stanford before his premature death while writing the little book from which I shall quote briefly.

Primary in liberal education, Hudson thought, is what he calls in good Shakespearean terms the "discourse of reason." The third of its three essentials is the "imaginative way of knowing." Politics needs literature as surely as literature interfuses politics. Wrote Hudson in the context and atmosphere of the Second World War:

> To recognize our emotional drives, to be aware of their force in directing and even methodizing our thought, to make allowance for them but on no account to deny that they exist or to be deceived as to their force and direction—this is to minimize, if not to cancel out, the famous dangers of emotional thinking. . . . I would point out that you can never possess any truth except by imagining it—or, as it is sometimes put, by realizing it.[11]

Likewise, in Trilling's interpretation, John Stuart Mill "understood from his own experience that the imagination was properly the joint possession of the emotions and the intellect, that it was fed by the emotions and without it the intellect withers and dies, that without it the mind cannot work and properly conceive itself."[12] That idea Hudson would recognize, and no doubt Trilling did also, as the underlying concept of Francis Bacon's notion of the "duty and office of rhetoric": to bring reason to the aid of imagination for the better moving of the will.

That area of discourse where the intellect and the emotions bestir each other in the exploration of opinion, of judgment, of social action is the characteristic common ground of literature and politics. It is the traditional ground of oratory and of those lesser grades of discourse which do not rise to the imaginative vigor of DeQuincey's "literature of power." But likewise, we are arguing, it is the ground of much that we know to be poetry, or at least *belles lettres*. Hence with a final draught upon Lionel Trilling, I shall turn to my concluding and corollary subject—that branch of theory, of doctrine, of learning which has as its chief concern, according to Bryant, "adjusting ideas to people and people to ideas," the "rationale of the informative and suasory in discourse."[13] In "The Meaning of a Literary Idea," Trilling observes:

> Of late years criticism has been much concerned to insist on the indirection and the symbolism of the language of poetry. I do not doubt that the language of poetry is very largely that of indirection and symbolism. But it is not only that. Poetry is closer to rhetoric than we today are willing to admit. . . . And those poets of our time who make

the greatest impress upon us are those who are most aware of rhetoric [though they would not *name* it!], which is to say, of the intellectual content of their work. [14]

At last have I begun using the word which has been implicit from the first sentence; and one wonders how I have so long stayed away from—*rhetoric*. I have not, really; and now I will no longer stay from it even verbally—for the theory of literature-politics in discourse is rhetoric.

All literature of affirmation and instigation and inculcation in its affirming and instigating and inculcating operations is rhetorical—from light minimal coaxing in "O come with me and be my love" to the full polemic of Demosthenes against Aeschines—and it is not studied to *most* effect until it is studied in the rhetorical mode—in the *rhetorical idiom*. It is to be studied in many ways by many sets of principles, but it must be studied, it seems to me, as directed discourse, or at least as composition involving significant external dynamics, intentional or not, and not merely as discourse having internal structure.

The post-Aristotelian writers on poetry appropriated and adapted most of their theory and principles from the only extensive systematic doctrines of composition which existed—the works of the rhetoricians, the teachers of speaking. And significant in this appropriated doctrine was the formulation of the ends of poetry—to teach, to delight, and (often) to move—in Horace, for example, and more especially in his successors for close to two thousand years. We recognize, of course, on the part of the critics if not of the poets, that there is a lack of philosophical depth, a naiveté in the use of the teach, delight, and move formula, from which only recently (as one reckons time in the history of thought) have we begun to be liberated. Why, then, should I try to put us back into bondage to it? That is far from my wish, nor would I be likely to succeed. I would suggest only that the naiveté consists in unsure grasp of the complexity and subtlety of the social mission and societal impact of literature. It does not lie in the basic assumption that such a mission and such impact are likely to be involved in the *consequences* of literary creation even when not intentionally involved in the *impulse* of such creation. Aristotle related rhetoric to the ethical side of politics—to the dynamics of the good man and the good society. Literature is inextricable from those dynamics. Plato in the *Phaedrus* called rhetoric the art of enchanting the soul with words; it might be thought folly to deny this function to literature—even *qua* literature. The distinctive function which Bacon assigned to rhetoric, as I have remarked, is to bring reason (note the order) to the aid of imagination for the better moving of the will. If works in which this function plays a substantial part were to that extent excluded from literature, or lost by default to psychology, behavioral science, sociology, anthropology, or semantics, we should mangle and deform most of the monuments of our inheritance.

Be that as it may, why choose to make an issue before such an audience as this of the area of study between the standard disciplines of literature and history, why presume to call for the reunion of wisdom and eloquence? Where rhetoric, literature, and philosophy gather together (even in unbalanced numbers)—what could be a better place? Like Francis Bacon, we are those among the learned who should search out and repair the deficiencies in humane learning, should detect and close the fissures which appear in the solid structure of liberal education and scholarship in consequence of the shifting masses of political fashion and social necessity. Like many members of this audience, faculty and student, I have busied my mind much from time to time about the compartmentalizing of university study and the consequent neglected consideration—that is, systematic and head-on consideration—of certain aspects of the operations of the human spirit which seem to be important. One of these characterizes that province of humanistic learning where literature and politics, where art and social dynamics interfuse.

A number of years ago I spoke at a conference devoted to the theme of the future of the humanities. (Who in university work has not, in one way or another, got embroiled in that controversy?) The result was a little piece in which I spoke of the fictions men live by and the frauds they live under.[15] The first, the fictions, are those ideas, those intellecutal and perhaps ethical concepts, what I think Trilling may have meant by those "sentiments," which we generate and incarnate through the discipline of study, in an active synthesis of intellect, imagination, emotion, and will—those imaginative inventions which since ancient times have been seen as the unique constructive ideas flowering in all true works of the fecund human spirit. The others, the frauds, are all those *erzatz* conceptions, those sterile, facile ideologies rather than ideas, those robot assemblages of motivations, which we too often embrace through pseudo-thought, ignorance, and impotence as substitutes for the struggle of creation.

I think now, as I thought then, that the principal task of sustaining productive learning in this area devolves upon the study of literature in the broad conception of it which I have been using (which would include the film and television as well as the live drama), because the ultimate scope of literary study especially, along with history and philosophy—that is, the ultimate scope of humanities—encompasses man at his best in his *total, live, active, relevant context.* That context is of the past as well as the present. Hence, it seems to me that in addition to preserving their age-old devotion to the rudiments of resourceful communication, the humanities must continue to revive their traditional concern with man exploiting *all* the resources of language to discipline the ideas and the motives and to guide the behavior of his fellows.

That is why I have undertaken over a period of years to present to colleagues and students a case for rhetorical consideration of literature as *one* important phase of study for *some* of us *some* of the time. I must confess that the undertaking has not been blessed with sudden and complete success—at least with respect to the sense of *rhetorical* which I wished to validate.

Since the revival of historical and critical interest in formal rhetoric, that is, in the contents of the books called *rhetorics*, in literary study, especially in Renaissance studies, there is no serious problem of establishing rhetoric as a study of imagery and literary form. It is there and it is rampant. Work by such scholars as Croll, Rosemund Tuve, William Wimsatt, Donald Lemen Clark, Rosalie Colie, and a dozen others has contributed invaluably to the sophistication of literary study—to the explication of texts, to the "reading" of poems, to the enriching of our knowledge of the atmosphere out of which literary works are born. It is a big task, furthermore, to show fully and subtly, on *all levels*, how a poem is made. And to the rationale of much of this undertaking it would be useless to deny the label rhetoric. It is a big task also, and a highly important one, to show fully and subtly, on *all levels*, how a poem, or any other discourse, *works*—to what ends, intended or unintended, and by what means it operates on the readers, the audience—how it manages to realize such potential as it exhibits and what the quality of that potential is.

This also is the province of rhetoric, and perhaps a more distinctive province than examining literary practice against the measures of literary precept and literary tradition. At least so thought that group of scholars and teachers who, returning to the rhetoric of Aristotle, Cicero, Plato, Quintilian, Saint Augustine, Thomas Wilson, Blair, Campbell, and the rest, effected a revival of rhetorical studies in the 1920s in the departments of public speaking, classics, and English. They turned to rhetoric, deserted, or at least strangely confined as it was, as the earlier Renaissance turned to ancient Greece, for the old-new ideas; and, as Hudson said, they found in rhetoric the organon of the humane studies. Their teaching in the classroom, their educational philosophies, their scholarly study and writing were all directed by the strong impetus better to comprehend and fulfill the requirements of the educated man active in a civilized political society. Hence, like James A. Winans in his textbook of 1915,[16] they sought in their teaching to rekindle the traditional principles of the ancients by breeding upon the classic stock the modern psychology of William James or Kafka and the political outlook of Jeffersonian, Wilsonian democratic society. As Everett L. Hunt put it:

> If we can keep as basic our conception that the humanities embrace whatever contributes to the making of free and enlightened choices, whether it be knowledge scientific, sociological, or poetic, and that in addition to adequate knowledge of all the alternatives there must be imagination to envisage all the possibilities and sympathy to make some of the options appeal to the emotions and powers of the will, we can see that rhetoric is an essential instrument for the enterprises of the human spirit.[17]

If coaxed or encouraged, Hunt could be tempted, I think, to add that all this virtue may be claimed for rhetoric (rhetoric not as digests of devices but as a mode of approaching the phenomena of discourse) not because rhetoric comprehends all knowledge and all learning—even if Cicero's orator seems to—but because rhetoric provides the rationale for organizing and directing through discourse all relevant knowledge and learning towards social enlightenment and social control.

This is a tough order, to be sure, and I know that its importance is far from proved to your satisfaction (unless you were a believer before we began). I would like to leave it for your brooding consideration, however, and to add only a final comment. As far as this lecture is concerned, you may now see why a consideration of literature and politics turns into a new call for the reunion of wisdom and eloquence, for what Wayne Booth calls the *rhetorical stance* in the teaching and criticism of discourse, and why at the end we may think back and see the meaning of our beginning with Winston Churchill and Edmund Burke.

Contributors

Lloyd F. Bitzer is a professor of communication arts at the University of Wisconsin and past president of the Speech Communication Association. He is a contributor to and co-editor of *The Prospect of Rhetoric*, a book reporting the work of some forty scholars involved in the National Developmental Project on Rhetoric. Editor of an edition of George Campbell's *The Philosophy of Rhetoric*, he is author of influential articles appearing in *Quarterly Journal of Speech* and *Philosophy and Rhetoric* and is a member of the editorial board of the latter journal.

Wayne C. Booth is Pullman Professor of English at the University of Chicago. He is author of *The Rhetoric of Fiction, Now Don't Try to Reason with Me, A Rhetoric of Irony,* and *Modern Dogma and the Rhetoric of Assent,* as well as editor of and contributor to *The Knowledge Most Worth Having.* He is co-editor of *Critical Inquiry* and a member of the editorial board of *Philosophy and Rhetoric.*

Donald C. Bryant is Carver Professor Emeritus at the University of Iowa. A former editor of *Quarterly Journal of Speech*, he is a member of the editorial board of *Philosophy and Rhetoric*. He has written extensively on Edmund Burke and eighteenth-century parliamentary speakers, has edited and contributed to *The Rhetorical Idiom* and *Papers in Rhetoric and Poetic*, and is author of *Rhetorical Dimensions in Criticism*. He is a past president of the Speech Communication Association.

Kenneth Burke taught for several years at Bennington College and has been a visiting professor at various colleges and universities. Since the publication of *Counter-Statement* in 1931, he has been widely recognized in the United States and abroad as a literary critic. His interest in communication and rhetoric is evident in all of his books, most particularly in *Permanence and Change, Grammar of Motives, Rhetoric of Motives, The Rhetoric of Religion,* and *Language as Symbolic Action.*

Henry W. Johnstone, Jr., is a professor of philosophy at the Pennsylvania State University. He is author of numerous articles on the role of argumentation in philosophy and of the books *Philosophy and Argument* and *The Problems of the Self*. With Maurice Natanson, he is a contributor to and co-editor of *Philosophy, Rhetoric, and Argumentation*. He was for the first nine years of its existence editor of *Philosophy and Rhetoric* and is now a member of the editorial board.

Maurice Natanson is a professor of philosophy at Yale University. He is author of numerous articles on existentialism and phenomenology. Along with his specialization in philosophy has been his interest in literature and in rhetoric. He is author of articles in *Quarterly Journal of Speech*; a contributor to and co-editor of *Philosophy, Rhetoric, and Argumentation*; and a member of the editorial board of *Philosophy and Rhetoric*.

Notes

Preface

1. Donald C. Bryant essay in this volume, p.103

2. Ibid., p.107

3. Kenneth Burke, "Irony sans Rust," *The New Republic*, 6 and 13 July 1974, p. 25.

4. Wayne C. Booth essay in this volume, p.11

5. Booth, *A Rhetoric of Irony* (Chicago: University of Chicago Press, 1974), p. xiii.

6. Bryant, *Rhetorical Dimensions in Criticism* (Baton Rouge: Louisiana State University Press, 1973), p. 20. See also Walter J. Ong, *Rhetoric, Romance, and Technology* (Ithaca: Cornell University Press, 1971), p. 2; and Caroll C. Arnold, "Oral Rhetoric, Rhetoric, and Literature," *Philosophy and Rhetoric*, 1 (Fall 1968): 191-210.

Wayne C. Booth

1. *Penguin Island* (Paris: Calmann-Lévy, 1908), bk. 4, chap. 4.

2. *Geraldine Bradshaw* (London: Barker, 1964), p. 98.

3. As reprinted in E. B. White, *The Second Tree from the Corner* (New York: Harper & Row, 1954), pp. 112-13.

4. *A Backward Glance*, (New York: Appleton, 1934; London: Constable, 1972), p. 173.

Kenneth Burke

1. Lincoln: University of Nebraska Press, 1974.

2. I. A. Richards, *The Philosophy of Rhetoric* (New York: Oxford University Press, 1936); Colin Murray Turbayne, *The Myth of Metaphor* (New Haven: Yale University Press, 1962); and Kenneth Burke, *Permanence and Change* (Indianapolis: Bobbs-Merrill, 1965; originally published New York: New Republic, 1935). These three books are referred to frequently throughout the essay. When citations are made in the text, either title or name of author appears in proximity to appropriate page numbers.

3. I omit my references to examples because so embarrassingly much in the interim has been put forward more thoroughly and more accurately. In particular I would refer to the essay by George de Santillana on "The Development of Rationalism and Empiricism," 1941, *International Encyclopedia of Unified Sciences*, vol. 2, no. 8.

4. Or see, in *Language as Symbolic Action* (pp. 73-74), my "contextual" comments on a possible Freudian "primal" dog; and in the same book, the essay "What Are the Signs of What?: A Theory of Entitlement," where I build around some quasi-Spinozistic terms for "raccoon," as contrasted with a sheerly "lexical" definition. Or, I write here, in keeping with Richards's observation (p. 32) that "the familiar sense of 'context' can be extended . . . to include the circumstances under which anything was written or said; wider still to include, for a work in Shakespeare, say, the other known uses of the word about that time, wider still finally to include anything whatever about the period, or about anything else which is relevant to our interpretation of it," though his particular use of the term is to be "none of these."

The section in my *Grammar of Motives* on "Scope and Reduction," particularly the discussion of "circumference," worries a lot with related problems of extension— and I still go on lamenting that no one, to my knowledge, has considered my application of such thinking to the dialectic of the U.S. Constitution. For instance, the author whom I have quoted on "legal reasoning" told me that he had read but the first part of my *Grammar* before writing his excellent book. And thus, although he is hitting all around what I call the "Constitution-behind-the-Constitution" (that is to say, the extraconstitutional *context* in which the Constitution was enacted and gets variously reenacted as that context changes, with corresponding changes of interpretation, by reason of what I call the "scene-act-ratio") in his book that dimension is never discussed head on. Subsequently, however, the needed kind of consideration is to be found to perfection in a work, *The Supreme Court and Social Science*, by Paul L. Rosen (Urbana: University of Illinois Press, 1972), albeit it arrived at by a route of its own. When reading these two books, I as it were cry out, "If I but had them when I made my unprofessional foray into the dialectic of what I called our Constitution's many conflicting 'wishes' (which Dr. Levi refers to in terms of conflicting 'ideals')." But I don't feel so bad as I once did. For although, to my knowledge, no reviewer in English has ever discussed the implication of my notions about context, situation, and circumference or scope of the scene in which an act gets constitutionally enacted, I have found a most surprising and gratifying ally; namely, a French scholar (Professor Charles Roig, now at the University of Geneva) who not only translated my talk on constitutional "principles" or "wishes" into terms of *principes* and *volontés*, but whose modes of presentation show how such notions can be applied to the equivalent of a Constitution in France. He has since published his analysis as a monograph, *Symboles et société: Une introduction à la politique des symboles d'après l'oeuvre de Kenneth Burke* (Bern, Frankfurt am Main, Las Vegas: Peter Lang, 1977).

Recently, in another connection, I summed it all up thus, with regard to a notable change in the membership of the Supreme Court (to match Roosevelt's policies) and a notable change now that has taken place under Nixon: Such developments amount to a reordering among the priorities of the Constitution's principles, which represent many conflicting "ideals," or as I said "wishes." (Elsewhere I have suggested that the many conflicting principles or rules or ideals or wishes embodied in our Constitution are analogous to Freud's notion of the id, that is but a grab-bag of wishes, regardless of how well or badly, in the realm of a patient's experience, they can get along with one another.) Since, in effect, a change in the relative rating among the wishes assigns them different ratings up and down the scale of priorities, such shifts are brought about with our constitutional means by shifts in the membership of the Supreme Court itself. Thus, Roosevelt's Court replaced a stress upon property rights by a stress upon civil rights. And now presumably the changes of membership in Nixon's Court will take us from civil rights to "law and order" (in relation such "extraconstitutional" or "environmental" things or conditions as police powers, data banks, inflation, cross-bussing, the so-called "energy crisis," measures involving the side-effects of technological pollution, and the growing global importance of multinational corporations, many of them bigger than all but the biggest governments.) And of course, we must not forget all that is implied in the fate-laden term President Eisenhower bequeathed us when saying farewell to his office: the "military-industrial complex."

5. Ithaca: Cornell University Press, 1962.

Maurice Natanson

1. *Nonverbal Communication: Notes on the Visual Perception of Human Relations* (Berkeley: University of California Press, 1969), p. 66.

2. Ibid., p. 71.

3. Ibid.

4. Ibid.

5. Ibid.

6. Trans. Bernard Frechtman (New York: Philosophical Library, 1949), p. 19.

7. Ibid., p. 12.

8. Ibid., pp. 13-14.

9. "Some Remarks on 'Literature and Reality,'" *Field*, Fall 1970 (published by Oberlin College).

10. Boston: Houghton Mifflin, 1941, p. 238.

11. *Kierkegaard* 2 vols. (New York: Harper Torchbooks, 1962), 2: 630.

12. *Russell Remembered* (London: Oxford University Press, 1970), p. 92.

13. "Jaspers' Relation to Max Weber," in *The Philosophy of Karl Jaspers*, ed. Paul Arthur Schilpp (New York: Tudor, 1957), pp. 371-72.

14. Karl Jaspers, "Reply to My Critics," ibid., p. 855.

15. Manasse, ibid., p. 390.

16. Ibid.

Henry W. Johnstone, Jr.

1. *Protagoras* 361A.

2. See Henry W. Johnstone, Jr., "Argumentation and Inconsistency," *Revue Internationale de Philosophie* 15, no. 4 (1961): 353-65.

3. See Johnstone, "Controversy and the Self," *Kantstudien* 58, no. 1 (1967): 22-32. (Reprinted with some revisions as chap. 10 of *The Problem of the Self* [University Park: Pennsylvania State University Press, 1970]).

4. See Johnstone, *Philosophy and Argument* (University Park: Pennsylvania State University Press, 1959), chap. 4.

5. See ibid., pp. 60-61.

6. Immanuel Kant, *Foundations of the Metaphysics of Morals*, trans. Lewis White Beck (New York: The Bobbs-Merrill Company, Inc., 1959), p. 22.

7. See Don M. Burks, "Persuasion, Self-Persuasion, and Rhetorical Discourse," *Philosophy and Rhetoric* 3 (1970): 109-19.

8. See *The Problem of the Self* (cited in n. 3), chap. 9.

9. It is undoubtedly too broad a definition of rhetoric to say simply that it evokes consciousness. So, for example, does music. But it does seem a necessary condition of the rhetorical act that it evoke consciousness.

10. See Johnstone, "The Relevance of Rhetoric to Philosophy and of Philosophy to Rhetoric," *Quarterly Journal of Speech* 52 (1966): 41-46, especially 41.

11. See Johnstone, "Rhetoric and Communication in Philosophy," in *Perspectives in Education, Religion, and the Arts* (Albany: State University of New York Press, 1970), pp. 351-64.

12. Ludwig Wittgenstein, *Tractatus Logico-Philosophicus*, trans. Pears and McGuinness (London: Routledge and Kegan Paul), 4:112.

13. See Johnstone, "Rationality and Rhetoric in Philosophy," *Quarterly Journal of Speech*, 59 (1973): 381-89.

14. Georg Hegel, *The Logic of Hegel*, trans. William Wallace, 2nd. ed. (Oxford, 1892), p. 158.

15. Ibid., p. 161.

Lloyd F. Bitzer

1. *Gorgias,* trans. Jowett, p. 482.

2. *Our Public Life* (Carbondale: Southern Illinois University Press, Arcturus edition, 1966), p. 196.

3. Chicago: Swallow Press, 1927. Page references to this work are enclosed in parentheses and inserted in the text.

4. *Personal Knowledge: Towards a Postcritical Philosophy* (Chicago: University of Chicago Press, 1958), p. 343.

5. Ibid., p. 375.

6. *The Public Philosophy* (New York: Mentor, 1956), p. 95.

Donald C. Bryant

1. "Rhetorical Dimensions in Criticism," in *Rhetorical Dimensions in Criticism* (Baton Rouge: Louisiana State University Press, 1973), pp. 28-29.

2. "The Literary Criticism of Oratory" (1925), in *The Rhetorical Idiom*, ed. Donald C. Bryant (Ithaca: Cornell University Press, 1958), p. 41.

3. For example, "A Concept of Eloquence," *Rhetorical Dimensions*, p. 136.

4. Ibid.

5. "Uses of Rhetoric in Criticism," in *Papers in Rhetoric and Poetic*, ed. Donald C. Bryant (Iowa City: University of Iowa Press, 1965), p. 13.

6. *The Works of . . . Edmund Burke*, 12 vols. (Boston: Little, Brown, 1894), 2: 105-06, 116-17.

7. Northrop Frye, *Anatomy of Criticism* (Princeton: Princeton University Press, 1957), p. 245.

8. *Papers in Rhetoric and Poetic*, p. 14.

9. John Morley, "Address at the Mansion House," *Pall Mall Gazette*, 28 February 1887, p. 12.

10. *The Liberal Imagination* (New York: Viking Press, 1950), p. xi.

11. Hoyt H. Hudson, *Educating Liberally* (Stanford: Stanford University Press, 1945), pp. 63, 57.

12. Trilling, p. xiv.

13. Donald C. Bryant, "Rhetoric: Its Functions and Its Scope," *Quarterly Journal of Speech* 39 (1953): 413; "Rhetoric: Its Functions and Its Scope *Rediviva*," *Rhetorical Dimensions*, p. 14.

14. Trilling, p. 290.

15. "Whither the Humanities?" *Quarterly Journal of Speech* 42 (1956): 363-66.

16. James A. Winans, *Public Speaking* (New York: Century Co., 1915).

17. *The Rhetorical Idiom*, p. 4.

The text of Rhetoric, Philosophy, and Literature: An Exploration *was set in Palatino typefaces by ProText Conversion Service of Indianapolis, Indiana. The book was printed by Thomson-Shore, Inc., of Dexter, Michigan on seventy-pound white Tiara Vicksburg vellum and casebound in Joanna Arrestox. David Brannan, graphic designer with the Purdue University Press, designed both the book and the dust jacket. Verna Emery, managing editor of the Press, was editorial and production supervisor.*